The desire to take chances is innate in humanity–primitive or civilized. Astrology, the oldest science of the world, has outlined the proper courses for people to follow for thousands of years. There is a time and a place for all things, and no more practical science in the world can be applied to mankind's daily affairs than the Science of Astrology and Numerology. If people must speculate, this book will be of immense value to anyone by showing them how to combine the laws that rule and regulate the universe with their own judgement. Accurate judgement is necessary for the success of any enterprise and by combining this with the fundamental laws of cause and effect, a greater measure of success can be achieved.

WONDER OF NUMBERS

(INCLUDING WAYS TO WIN IN ANY SPECULATION & SIMPLE TECHNIQUES TO IMPROVE YOUR PERSONALITY USING THE SCIENCES OF NUMEROLOGY AND ASTROLOGY)

Pt. Gopal Sharma, B.E.

DIAMOND BOOKS

Publisher : Diamond Pocket Books (P) Ltd.
X-30, Okhla Indl. Area, Phase-II,
New Delhi-110020

Phone : **011-40712200**

E-mail : **sales@dpb.in**

Website : **www.diamondbook.in**

Distributor : Institute of Vaastu & Joyful Living
B-292, Saraswati Vihar,
Outer Ring Road, Pitam Pura
New Delhi-110034
Phones: 27030966/67, 27020736
Fax : 27028228

E-mail : ptgopal@yahoo.com

website : www.panditgopalsharma.com

WONDERS OF NUMBERS

by *Pt. Gopal Sharma, B.E.*

DEDICATED

To

Late Niranjan - Pithadheshwar
Acharya Mahamandleshwar
Yatinder Shri 1008
Swami Krishnanand
Giriji Maharaj
who laid his life
for propagating

'TRUTH'

Pt. GOPAL SHARMA, B.E. being honoured by other legends i.e. Dr. Sukhdev Chaturvedi, Sh. Jai Prakash Lal Dhage Wale & Sh. Arun Bansal, President AIFA during a seminar at HOTEL LE-MERIDIEN, NEW DELHI.

Pt. Gopal Sharma being honoured by Shri. G.V.G Krishnamurthy Ex. Chief Election Commissioner, Pt. Jai Prakash Sharma (Lal-Dhage Wale), Shri Arun Bansal & Shri.C.L. Panchal from Bhopal.

About the Author

Born in a renowned family of vedic scholars & spiritual healers, Vaastu Engineer Pt. Gopal Sharma is a luminary in many fields. Pt.Gopal Sharma was initiated into spiritualism by late Niranjan - Phithatheshwar Acharya Mahamandleshwar Yatinder Swami Krishnanand Giriji Maharaj in 1968. During next five years of study in Delhi College of Engineering, he developed keen interest in various facets of Vedanta, Graphology, Palmistry and Astrology. It was sharpened by deep study, research work & through the blessings of great sages & saints during his extensive touring in various parts of the world.

His unique & imaginative contribution as a Development Engineer with Eicher group of companies from 1973 -1978 is still appreciated by the top brass of the group.

During his association for 12 years as a technical / economic advisor with a leading nationalised bank, he had been deeply involved in establishing / expansion and revival of numerous industrial enterprises.

He has been doing research & experiments on the basic principles of Vaastu for the use of common men and propagating this exhausitive art and ancient science of buildings exhibited in origional ancient texts by :

- ☆ Organising / contributing to various seminars and symposiums in various parts of the world.
- ☆ Regularly publishing useful information about these holistic subject in various newspapers and magazines.
- ☆ Delivering lectures and distributing write-ups in various get-together of architects, builders/developers, industrialists and also in the conferences organised by different NGO's like Rotary clubs, Lion's club etc.
- ☆ Giving spiritual counselling, Astro, Vaastu, Pyramidology & Feng-Shui consultancy to the various segments of society.

He is an eminent technical / management & financial consultant for many large industrial/business houses. He is currently specialising in advanced research on various aspects of Energy-Flow; being an effective combination of Bio-electro-magnetism, Indian-Geomancy, Chinese-Vaastu / Feng-Shui, and pyramidology.

Besides Governor of All India Federation of Astrologer's societies (regd.), Delhi Pt. Gopal sharma, B.E. is the founder President of Institute of Vaastu & Joyful Living. For years he continues to serve humanity; being the Chief Patron of Indian Astrologer Human Welfare Association & President of Parampara, a premier NGO of the country. He has also been felicitated with several medals and awards for painfully and selflessly promoting this edifice science to the masses.

Through the Head Office of the Institute at PITAMPURA & branch offices at Hyderabad, Singapore, Kuala Lumpur (Malaysia) & New Jersey(USA) Pt. Gopal Sharma is presently adding peace, prosperity & happiness in the lives of people by consultancy & courses of Astrology, Palmistry, Vaastu / Feng-Shui, Pyramidology, Reiki & Meditation by correspondence & regular/part-time classes. Even free service is regularly provided to those who can't afford on every Monday & Thursday between 3 to 5 p.m. Pt. Gopal Sharma was officially consulted by the Government of U.P. for planning the entire TRONICA CITY; the prestigious 1600 acre residential cum industrial complex; which proved a phenomenal success.He has to his credit 33 best selling books in Hindi, English, German & French. Based on his published material he has been recently awarded the DOCTORATE IN VAASTU SCIENCE by the Open University at Sri Lanka.

Pt. Gopal Sharma B.E.
Institute of Vaastu & Joyful Living
B-292, Saraswati Vihar,
Outer Ring Road,
New Delhi- 110034
PH : 27020736, 27030966, 27030967,
FAX : 27028228
CELL : 9810054314, 20065048
Web : www.panditgopalsharma.com
e-mail :ptgopal@yahoo.com, vastuvocational@vsnl.net

CONTENTS

HOW TO WIN AT ANY KIND OF SPECULATION USING THE SCIENCES OF NUMEROLOGY AND ASTROLOGY

INTRODUCTION

In every human mind is a spark of the gambling instinct—a desire to take chances that aforesaid the thrill of gaining or losing in such a venture. Life itself is a speculation : a child is born—perhaps it will live and perhaps it will not; a merchant opens a business—perhaps he will succeed or perhaps he won't; an aviator takes a long flight—perhaps he will make a safe landing or not, etc. The desire to take chances is innate in all kind of humanity, primitive or civilized.

Homi Jahangir Bhabha said, "Astrology is Astronomy brought to earth and applied to the affairs of men." Astrology, the oldest science in the world, has outlined the proper courses for people to follow for many thousands of years. "There is a time and a place for all things," and no more practical science in the world can be applied to mankind's daily affairs than the science of Astrology and Numerology.

Varah-Mihir, the great astrologer and philosopher of ancient times, has said, "Judgment must be regulated by yourself, as well as by the science—it is advantageous to make choice of days and hours at a time constituted by the nativity."

While the author of this book does not recommend nor encourage promiscuous gambling in any form, he is mindful of the fact that so long as human beings are constituted as they are at present, they are going to indulge in some form of speculation, whether it be for pleasure and amusement, starting business, taking trips, buying and selling stocks, real estate, commodities, etc. Hence, if people MUST speculate, this book will be of value to anyone by showing them how to combine the law that rule and regulate the universe with their own judgment. You will remember that accurate judgment is also necessary for the success of any enterprise, yet by combining this with the fundamental laws of cause and effect outlined by the science of the universe herein treated, a greater measure of success may be attained than by attempting things at a time that might prove to be very inopportune.

We present this information for what is may be worth. It may appeal to you as a pastime flavored with the thrill of a test of skill tempered by your judgment. We would have all readers pleased and interested. But none enslaved by it.

For those who have read the contents of this book with interest and wish to test it out for results, we suggest that you keep tab on the schedule outlined; it will save you considerable money and bring excellent results.

"The lucky have whole days, and these they choose. The unlucky have but hours—and these they lose."

LUCKY DAY
YOUR FORTUNATE NUMBERS

These methods, based on the Science of Numerology, are different for every person. The author has spent many years studying the occult meaning of numbers, and while we do not guarantee results, many use them with great success.

WHAT YOU MUST KNOW

FIRST : Learn how to tell magic time. Numbers inside the circle represent A.M.—Just like a watch. Numbers outside circle represent the time after noon. ALWAYS NOTE HOUR.

MAGIC TIME

A.M. 1-2-3-4-5-6-7-8-9-10-11-12

P.M. 13-14-15-16-17-18-19-20-21-22-23-24

SECOND : Note the day of week. Monday is 1; Tuesday is 2; Wednesday is 3; Thursday is 4; Friday is 5; Saturday is 6; Sunday is 7.

THIRD : Count the number of letters in your name. Example : Prem Chand has four letters in the first name and five in his second name. 4 plus 5 equals 9. This number will always be lucky for Prem Chand.

FOURTH : A lucky number when found by combining the values of the days when born. Example : If you were born on June 25 (June is the 6th month), combine 6 and 25. Thus 625 or 67. Add these figures : 6 plus 2 plus 5 equals 13. Add again 1 plus 3 equals 4. This gives four magic numbers, all with same strength : 625,67,13 & 4. Use the one that suits you best. Jan equals 1; Feb 2; March 3; April 4; May 5; June 6; July 7; Aug. 8; Sept.9; Oct.10; Nov.11 (or 2) Dec. 12 or (3).

FOUR METHODS FOR USING YOUR FORTUNATE NUMBERS

1. ***THE MAGIC HOUR***—Use the number of the day of the week and the number of the hour at which you play or bet. Example : Suppose it is 4 P.M. on Friday (see clock). 4 P.M. is 16 O'clock; Friday is 5, Combine these to make 165 or 75. Then add 1 plus 6 plus 5 equals 12. Add again, 1 plus 2 equals 3. This gives four magic numbers : 165, 75, 12, 3 with the same strength. Use the one that suits you best.
2. ***STRIKE THE KEYNOTE*** : Use the number of letter in your name and the hour of play. Suppose Prem Chand (9) wants a Lucky Number at 8 P.M. Combine 9 and 20 to make 920. Add these : 9 plus 2 plus 0 equals 11. Add again, 1 plus

1 equals 2. This gives four magic numbers : 920, 29, 11, 2. Use the one that suits you best.

3. ***YOUR PINACLE OF SUCCESS*** : Use the number of the day on which you were born and the number of the month. Suppose you were born on Aug. 24th. Combine 24 and 8. This gives 248 or 68. Add 2 plus 4 plus 8 equals 14. Add again 1 plus 4 equals 5. This gives you four Lucky Numbers of the same magic power : 248, 68, 14, 5.

4. *LADY LUCK METHOD* : Count the number of letters in your sweetheart's name and combine with the number of letters in your own name. Example : Rajneesh Kumar (13 letters) and Prem Chand (9 letters) makes 139 or 47. Add these : 1 plus 3 plus 9 equals 13. Add again, 1 plus 3 equals 4. This gives you four Lady Luck numbers : 139, 49, 13, 4. Use the one that suits the occasion best.

NOTE : If you want more than one Lucky Number in a day, combine your Lady Luck number with the hour. Example : At 20 O'clock (8 P.M.), combine Rajneesh Kumar (13) with the Prem Chand (9) : 20, 139. Add these to suit your convenience. ALWAYS NOTE THE HOUR. The time figure changes only when the hour changes. Adding, transposing or combining a magic number does not alter its strength. Example : 165, 75, 12 or 3. Also a zero in a number can be used or not –200, 20, 2.

LUCKY DAYS-ARIES

FOR ALL THOSE BORN BETWEEN MARCH 21ST AND APRIL 20TH

Astrology indicates the exact periods when you should speculate and when you should not do so. The Earth going through the twelve signs of the Zodiac forms certain configurations which indicate your prospects in any game of chance. Thus, you have regular periods every year when you may win or lose. It is up to you to make use of this information. In order to make this reading the most accurate, your sign has been divided into three sections. The division, by decanate, gives you about ten days which are influenced by the Sun's transits.

IF YOU ARE BORN BETWEEN MARCH 21st to 31st. You may speculate during the following periods, and may expect to win.

Junuary	21st	to	31st
May	21st	to	31st
July	23rd	to	3rd August
November	23rd	to	3rd December

From March 21 to 31st you will be tempted to speculate yet must determine for yourself whether or not this period is fortunate. Do not speculate from June 22nd to 2nd of July, September 23rd to 4th of October & December 22nd to 3rd of January of any year.

IF YOU ARE BORN BETWEEN APRIL 1st to 10th. You may speculate during the following periods of any year, and may expect to win :

February	1st	to	11th
June	1st	to	12 th

August	3rd	to	14th
December	2nd	to	13th

From April 1st to 12th you will also be tempted to speculate, yet you must find out for yourself whether or not you can win. Do not speculate from January 2nd to 23rd, July 2nd to 14th and October 3rd to 15th.

IF YOU ARE BORN BETWEEN APRIL 11th to 20th. You may speculate during the following periods of any year, and may expect to win :

February	9th	to	20th
June	10th	to	21th
August	12th	to	23rd
December	11th	to	13th

From April 10 to 20th you will also be tempted to speculate, yet must find out for yourself whether or not you can win. Do not speculate from January 12th to 19th, from July 13th to 23rd & October 14 to 23rd.

All Aries-born are inclined to take chances between July 22nd and August 23rd. When you speculate in cooperation with others, it would be advisable that your partner is born under one of the following signs :

Aquarius	Jan. 21st	to	Feb. 19th
Gemini	May 22nd	to	June 21st
Leo	July 24th	to	Aug. 23rd
Sagittarius	Nov. 23rd	to	Dec. 22nd
Libra	Sept. 24th	to	Oct. 23rd

IMPORTANT : **Read Page 64-67** for the cycles of JUPITER, which indicate your fortunate years. When under an adverse cycle, you are warned to be careful in speculating.

A small place for Pooja should be made north, east, north-east zone.

SPECIAL TIPS

- Those born between March 21st to March 28th will have better chances in speculation during the new moon.
- Those born between March 29th and April 5th will have better chances in speculation during the second quarter of the moon.
- Those born between April 6th and April 13th will have better chances in speculation during the full moon.
- Those born during April 14th and April 20th will have better chances in speculation during the fourth quarter of the moon.

NUMEROLOGY

According to the Science of Numerology, the Celestial Number of Aries is 7, Mars, the ruling planet of the sign has the Number 6 for its numerical value. Combining these two numbers we have 7 plus 6 which equals 13. This number must now be reduced to a single digit : therefore, 1 plus 3 equals 4. The Numbers 4 if then the key number of all persons born in Aries. Bear this in mind on all occasions. When you buy a ticket of any sort, see the Serial Number has 4 as the predominating number, Room Number 4 in a hotel, a Street Number containing a 4 several 4's, horse Number 4 in a race, player Number 4 in a sport game, a card that totals 4 in a card game, a 4 rolled with dice, 4 on a spin wheel, etc. are considered fortunate for you.

ILLUSTRATION : Suppose you have two cards in your hand; a ten-spot and a three-spot. 10 plus 3 equals 13, and 1 plus 3 equals 4. Therefore, such a hand of cards would be fortunate for you, or any other combination that could be reduced to 4. If you should have a combination that totals 31, that would also reduce to 4, because 3 plus 1 equals 4, etc. Use the same method of reduction to a single digit with other combinations.

FIND YOUR BEST DAYS FOR SPECULATION :

Any day of any month that totals 4 is considered fortunate for you : thus, the 13th, the 22nd and the 31st of a month because any of these dates reduced to a single digit make 4. The days of the month that are best for speculation are the 4th, 13th, 22nd and 31st. However, you should engage in speculation only in your proper months or periods as explained below.

PROPER HOURS FOR SPECULATION :

The proper hour for speculation is when your ruling planet is governing. Refer to your daily paper, almanac or calender to find the time of sunrise. These hours are the same every week, month and year. Only the time of sunrise changes.

HOURS FOR SPECULATION—Sunday : 7th, 14th, 21st hour after sunrise. Monday : 4th, 11th, 18th hour after sunrise. Tuesday : 1st, 8th, 15th, 22nd hour after sunrise. Wednesday : 5th, 12th, 19th hour after sunrise. Thursday : 2nd, 9th, 16th, 23rd hour after sunrise. Friday : 6th, 13th, 20th hour after sunrise. Saturday : 3rd, 10th, 17th, 24th hour after sunrise.

Activate North	**For**	**Better Career Planning**
Activate South	**For**	**Fame & Recognition**
Activate West	**For**	**Children's Luck**
Activate East	**For**	**Longevity & Confidence**

LUCKY DAYS—TAURUS

FOR ALL THOSE BORN BETWEEN APRIL 21ST TO MAY 21ST ANY YEAR

ASTROLOGY indicates the exact periods when you should speculate and when you should not do so. The Earth going through the Twelve signs of the Zodiac forms certain configurations which indicate your prospects in any game of chance. Thus you have regular periods every year when you will win or when you may lose and it is up to you to make use of this information. In order to make this reading the most accurate, your sign has been divided into three sections. The division, by decanate, gives you about ten days which are influenced by the Sun's transits.

IF YOU ARE BORN BETWEEN APRIL 21st to 30th and May 1st. You may speculate during the following periods and may expect to win :

February	20th	to	1st of March
June	22nd	to	3rd of July
August	24th	to	4th of September
December	23rd	to	3rd of January

From April 21st to May 2nd, you will also be tempted to speculate, yet must determine for yourself whether or not you can win. Do not speculate from January 21st to February 2nd, from July 24th to August 4th & from October 24th to November 3rd.

IF YOU ARE BORN BETWEEN MAY 2nd to 11th. You may speculate during the following periods, and may expect to win :

January	2nd	to	12th
March	1st	to	11th
July	2nd	to	13th
September	2nd	to	14th

From May 1st to 12th, you will also be tempted to speculate, yet must determine for yourself whether or not you can win. Do not speculate from February 1st to 11th, from August 2nd to 14th & from November 2nd to 13th.

IF YOU ARE BORN BETWEEN MAY 12th to 21st you may speculate during the following periods and may expect to win :

January	10th	to	20th
March	11th	to	20th
July	12th	to	23rd
September	12th	to	23rd

From May 10th to 21st, you will also be tempted to speculate, yet must determine for yourself whether or not you can win. Do not speculate from February 9th to 19th, from August 10th to 23rd & from November 11th to 23rd.

All Taurus-born are inclined to take chances between August 24th to September 23rd. When you speculate in cooperation with others, it would be advisable that your partner is born under one of the following signs :

Pisces	Feb. 20th	to	March 20th
Taurus	Apr. 21st	to	May 21st
Cancer	June 22nd	to	July 23rd
Virgo	Aug. 24th	to	Sept. 23rd
Scorpio	Oct 24th	to	Nov. 22nd
Capricorn	Dec. 23rd	to	Jan. 20th

IMPORTANT : **Read page 64-67** for the Cycles of Jupiter, which indicate your fortunate years. When under an Adverse Cycles, you are warned to be careful in you speculation.

SPECIAL TIPS

- Those born during April 21st and April 28th will have better chances in speculation during the new moon.
- Those born between April 19th to May 5th will have better chances in speculation during the second quarter of the moon.
- Those born during May 6th to May 14th will have better chances in speculation during the full moon.
- Those born between May 15th to May 21st will have better chances in speculation during the fourth quarter of the moon.
- NEARLY ALL CALENDARS GIVE THE FOUR QUARTERS OF THE MOON.

NUMEROLOGY

According to the Science of Numerology the Celestial Number of Taurus is 9. Venus, the ruling planet of this sign also has the number of 9. Combining these two numbers we have : 9 plus 9 which, equals 18. This number must now be reduced to a single digit therefore 1 plus 8 equals 9. The number 9 is the key number for all persons born in Taurus. Bear this in mind on all occasion. When you buy a ticket of any sort, see that the Serial Number has 9 as the predominating number. Room Number 9 in a hotel, a Street Number containing a 9 or several 9's, horse, Number 9 in a race. Player Number 9 in a sport game, cards that total 9 in a card game, a 9 rolled with dice, 9 on a spin wheel, etc. are considered fortunate for you.

ILLUSTRATION : Suppose you have two cards in your hand: a four-spot and a five-spot. Now 4 plus 5 equals 9, therefore such a hand of cards would be fortunate for you or any other combination that could be reduced to 9. If you should have a combination that totals 36, that would also reduce to 9, etc. Use the same method of reduction to a single digit with other combination.

FIND YOUR BEST DAYS OR SPECULATION:

Any day of the month that totals 9 is considered fortunate for you, thus : the 18th and 27th, because these dates reduce to a single digit making 9. The days of the month that are best for speculation are the 9th, 18th and 27th. However, you should engage in speculation only in your proper months or periods as explained below.

PROPER HOURS FOR SPECULATION :

The proper hour for speculation is when your ruling planet is governing. Refer to your daily paper, almanac or calender to find the time of sunrise. Then count the hours after sunrise. These hours are the same every week, month and year, only the time of sunrise changes.

HOURS FOR SPECULATION : Sunday : 2nd, 10th, 16th hour after sunrise. Monday : 6th, 13th, 20th hour after sunrise. Tuesday : 3rd, 8th, 15th, 24th hour after sunrise. Wednesday : 7th, 14th, 21st hour after sunrise. Thursday : 4th, 11th, 18th hour after sunrise, Friday : 1st, 8th, 15th, 22nd hour after sunrise, Saturday : 3th, 12th, 19th hour after sunrise.

LUCKY DAYS-GEMINI

FOR ALL THOSE BORN BETWEEN MAY 22ND TO JUNE 21ST

ASTROLOGY indicates the exact periods when you should speculate and when you should not do so. The Earth going through the Twelve signs of the Zodiac forms certain configurations which indicate your prospects in any game of chance. Thus you have regular periods every year when you will win or when you may lose and it is up to you to make use of this information. In order to make this reading the most accurate, your sign has been divided into three sections. This division by decanate, gives you about ten days which are influenced by the Sun's transits.

IF YOU ARE BORN BETWEEN MAY 22nd to 31st & JUNE 1st, you may speculate during the following periods, and may expect to win :

January	21st	to	30th
March	21st	to	31st
July	24th	to	3rd of August
September	23rd	to	3rd of October

From May 22nd to June 1st, you will also be tempted to speculate, yet must determine for yourself whether or not you can win. Do not speculate from February 20th to 29th, August 24th to 3rd to September & November 23rd to 2nd of December.

IF YOU ARE BORN BETWEEN JUNE 2nd to 11th, you may speculate during the following periods, and may expect to win:

January	31st	to	9 th February
April	1st	to	10th
August	4th	to	13th
October	4th	to	13th

From June 2nd to 11th, you will also be tempted to speculate, yet must determine for yourself whether or not you can win. Do not speculate from March 1st to 10th, September 4th to 13th & December 3rd to 12th.

IF YOU ARE BORN BETWEEN JUNE 12th to 21st, you may speculate during the following periods, and may expect to win:

February	10 th	to	19th
April	11th	to	20th
August	13th	to	23rd
October	14th	to	23rd

From June 12th to 21st, you will also be tempted to speculate, yet must determine for yourself whether or not you can win. Do not speculate from March 11th to 20th, September 13th to 23rd & December13th to 22th.

All Gemini-born are inclined to take chances between September 24th to October 23rd. When you speculate in cooperation with others, it would be advisable that your partner is born under one of the following signs :

Aquarius	Jan. 21st	to	Feb. 19th
Aries	Mar. 21st	to	Apr. 20th
Gemini	May 22nd	to	June 21st
Leo	July 24th	to	Aug. 23rd
Libra	Sept. 24th	to	Oct. 23rd
Sagittarius	Nov. 23rd	to	Dec. 22nd

IMPORTANT : **Read pages 64-67** for the Cycles of JUPITER, which indicate your fortunate years. When under an Adverse Cycle, you are warned to be most careful in your speculations, as it is a period when you will not be very lucky.

SPECIAL TIPS

- Those born between May 22nd and May 29th will have a better chance in speculation during the new moon.
- Those born between May 30th and June 6th will have a better chance in speculation during the second quarter of the moon.
- Those born between June 7th and June 14th will have a better chance in speculation during the full moon.
- Those born between June 15th and June 21st will have a better chance in speculation during the fourth quarter of the moon.
- NEARLY ALL CALENDARS GIVE THE FOUR QUARTERS OF THE MOON.

NUMEROLOGY

According to the Science of Numerology the Celestial Number of Gemini is 3. Mercury, the ruling planet of this sign has the numerical value of 4. Combining these two numbers we have 3 plus 4 which equals 7. The Number 7 is the key number for all persons born in Gemini. Bear this in mind on all occasions. When you buy a ticket of any sort, see that the Serial Number has 7 as the predominating number. Room number 7 in a hotel. A street number containing a 7, or Several 7's, Horse number 7 in a race, Player number 7 in a sport game, Cards that total 7 in a card game. A 7 rolled with dice, 7 on a spin wheel etc. are considered fortunate for you.

ILLUSTRATION : Suppose you have two cards in your hand: a three-spot. Now 3 plus 4 equals 7, therefore such a hand of cards would be fortunate for you, or any other combination that could be reduced to 7. If you should have a combination that totals 52, that will also reduce to 7. Use the same method of reduction to a single digit with other combinations.

FIND YOUR BEST DAYS FOR SPECULATION :

Any day of any month that totals 7 is considered fortunate for you, thus : the 16th, and the 25th because these dates when reduced to a single digit totals 7. The days of the month that are best for speculation are the 7th, 16th and 25th, however, you should engage in speculation only in your proper months or period as explained below.

PROPER HOURS FOR SPECULATION :

The proper hour for speculation is when your ruling planet is governing. Refer to your daily paper, almanac or calendar to find the time of sunrise, then count the hours after sunrise. These hours are the same every week, month, and year. Only the time of sunrise changes.

HOURS FOR SPECULATION—Sunday : 3rd, 10th, 17th, 24th hour after sunrise, Monday : 7th, 14th, 21st hour after sunrise. Tuesday : 4th, 11th, 18th hour after sunrise. Wednesday : 1st, 8th, 15th, 22nd hour after sunrise. Thursday : 5th, 12th, 19th hour after sunrise. Friday : 2nd, 9th, 16th, 23rd hour after sunrise. Saturday 6th, 13th, 20th hour after sunrise.

LUCKY DAYS—CANCER

FOR ALL THOSE BORN BETWEEN JUNE 22ND TO JULY 23RD

ASTROLOGY indicates the exact periods when you should speculate and when you should not do so. The Earth going through the twelve signs of the Zodiac forms certain configurations which indicate your prospects in any game of chance. Thus you have regular periods every year when you will win or when you may lose and it is up to you to make use of the information. In order to make this reading the most accurate, your sign has been divided into three sections. This division, by decanate, gives you about ten days which are influenced by the Sun's transits.

IF YOU ARE BORN BETWEEN JUNE 22nd to 30th & *JULY* 1st, 2nd. You may speculate during the following periods and may expect to win :

February	20th	to	29th
April	21st	to	1st of May.
August	24th	to	3rd of Sept.
October	24th	to	2nd of Nov.

From June 22nd to July 2nd, you will also be tempted to speculate, yet must determine for yourself whether or not you can win. Do not speculate from March 21st to 31st, September 24th to 3rd of October, and December 22nd to 31st.

IF YOU ARE BORN BETWEEN JULY 3rd to 13th, you may

speculate during the following periods, and may expect to win:

March	1st	to	10th
May	2nd	to	12th
Sept.	4th	to	13th
Nov.	3rd	to	12th.

From July 3rd to the 13th, you will also be tempted to speculate, yet must determine for yourself whether or not you can win. Do not speculate from April 1st to 10th, October 4th to 13th and January 1st to 12th.

IF YOU ARE BORN BETWEEN JULY 14th to 23rd. You may speculate during the following periods and may expect to win:

March	11th	to	20th
May	12th	to	21st
Sept.	14th	to	23rd
Nov.	13th	to	22nd

From July 3rd to the 13th, you will also be tempted to speculate, yet must determine for yourself whether or not you can win. Do not speculate from April 1st to 10th, October 4th to 13th and January 1st to 12th.

IF YOU ARE BORN BETWEEN JULY 14th to 23rd. You may speculate during the following periods and may expect to win:

March	11th	to	20th
May	12th	to	21st
Sept.	14th	to	23rd
Nov.	13th	to	22nd

From July 14th to 23rd, you will also be tempted to speculate, yet must determine from yourself whether or not you can win. Do not speculate from April 11th to 20th, October 13th to 23rd and January 10th to 20th.

All Cancer-born are inclined to take chance between October 24th to November 22nd. When you speculate in cooperation with others, it would be advisable that your partner is born under one of the following signs :

Pisces	Feb. 20th	to	March 20th
Taurus	Apr. 21st	to	May 21st
Cancer	June 22nd	to	July 23rd
Virgo	Aug. 24th	to	Sept. 23rd
Scorpio	Oct. 24th	to	Nov. 22nd
Capricorn	Dec. 23rd	to	Jan. 20th

SPECIAL TIPS

- Those born between June 22nd and June 29th will have better chances in speculating during the new moon.
- Those born between June 30th and July 7th will have better chances in speculation during the second quarter of the moon.
- Those born between July 8th and July 17th will have better chances in speculation during the full moon.
- Those born between July 18th and July 23rd will have better chances in speculation during the fourth quarter of the moon.
- NEARLY ALL CALENDARS GIVE THE FOUR QUARTERS OF THE MOON.

NUMEROLOGY

According to the science of Numerology the Celestial Number of Cancer is 8. The moon, the ruling planet of this sign, has the numerical value of 3. Combining these two numbers we have 8 plus 3, which equals 11. This must be reduced to a single digit, therefore, 1 plus 1 equals 2. The number 2 is the key number for all persons born in Cancer. Bear this in mind on all occasions. When you buy a ticket of any sort, see that the serial number has the predominating number 2 in it. Room number 2 in a hotel, a street number containing a 2 or several 2's, horse number 2 in a race, player number 2 in a sport game, cards that total 2 in a card game, a 2 rolled in dice, 2 on a spinwheel, etc., are considered fortunate for you.

ILLUSTRATION : Suppose you have two cards in your hand; a nine spot and a two spot. Now 9 plus 2 equals 11, and 11 when added (1 plus 1) equals 2. Therefore, such a hand would be fortunate for you, or any other combination of cards that could be added and reduced to 2. If you should have a combination that total 45, this would reduce to 2. Use the same method with other combination and totals.

FIND YOUR BEST DAYS FOR SPECULATION :

Any day of the any month that totals 2 is considered fortunate for you thus : 11th, 20th, 29th because these dates reduce to a single digit 2. Therefore, the days of the month that are best for speculation are 2nd, 11th, 20th and 29th, However, you should engage in speculation only in your proper months or periods as explained below.

PROPER HOURS FOR SPECULATION :

The proper hour for speculation is when your ruling planet is governing. Refer to your daily proper; almanac or calender to find the time of sunrise : then count the hours after sunrise. These hours are the same every week, month and year. Only the time of sunrise changes.

HOURS FOR SPECULATION—Sunday : 4th, 11th, 18th hour after sunrise. Monday : 1st, 8th, 15th, 22nd hour after sunrise. Tuesday : 5th, 12th, 19th hour after sunrise. Wednesday : 2nd, 9th, 16th, 23rd hour after sunrise. Thursday : 6th, 13th, 20th hour after sunrise. Friday : 3rd, 10th, 17th, 24th hour after sunrise. Saturday : 7th, 14th, 21st hour after sunrise.

Keep a Mirror, Wall-Clock, an Ornamental Fountain Aquarium/Picture or Painting of Moving Water without hills to activate *North-East* zone for Better Education & Knowledge. Photo of Golden Temple/Vrindavan Garden has been found very effective.

LUCKY DAY-LEO

FOR ALL THOSE BORN BETWEEN JULY 24TH TO AUGUST 23RD

ASTROLOGY indicates the exact periods when you should speculate and when you should not do so. The Earth going through the twelve signs of the Zodiac forms certain configurations which indicate your prospects in any game of chance. Thus you have regular periods every year when you will win or when you may lose and it is up to you to make use of this information. In order to make this reading the most accurate, your sign has been divided into three sections. This division, by decanate, gives about ten days which are influenced by the Sun's transit.

IF YOU ARE BORN BETWEEN JULY 24th to 31st & August 1st to 3rd. You may speculate during the following periods, and may expect to win :

March	21st	to	31st
May	22nd	to	1st of June
September	24th	to	3rd of Oct.
November	23rd	to	2nd of Dec.

From July 24th to August 5th you will also be tempted to speculate, yet must determine for yourself whether or not you can win. Do not speculate from January 21st to 30th, April 21st to 2nd of May and October 23rd to 3rd of November.

IF YOU WERE BORN BETWEEN AUGUST 4th, 5th, 6th, 7th, 8th, 9th, 10th, 11th, 12th, 13th. You may speculate during the following periods and may expect to win :

April	1st	to	11th
June	2nd	to	12th
October	3rd	to	13th
December	3rd	to	12th

From August 2nd to 14th, you will also be tempted to speculate, yet must determine for yourself whether or not you can win. Do not speculate from January 31st to February 10th, May 2nd to 12th and November 2nd to 13th.

IF YOU ARE BORN BETWEEN AUGUST 14th to 23rd, you may speculate during the following period and may expect to win :

April	10th	to	20th
June	12th	to	21st
October	13th	to	23rd
December	12th	to	22nd

From August 12th to 23rd you will also be tempted to speculate, yet must determine for yourself whether or not you can win. Do not speculate from February 12th to 19th, May 11th to 21st, and November 12th to 22nd.

All Leo-born are inclined to take chances between November 23rd and December 22nd. When you speculate in cooperation with others, it would be advisable that your partner is born under one of the following signs :

Aquarius	Jan. 21st	to	Feb. 19th
Aries	Mar. 21st	to	Apr. 20th
Gemini	May 22nd	to	June 21st
Leo	July 24th	to	Aug. 23rd
Libra	Sept. 24th	to	Aug. 23rd
Sagittarius Nov.	23rd	to	Dec. 22nd

IMPORTANT : **Read pages 64-67** for the Cycle of JUPITER, which indicates your fortunate years. When under an Adverse Cycle, you are warned to be most careful in your speculations, as it is a period when you will not be very lucky.

SPECIAL TIPS

- Those born between July 24th and July 31st will have better chances in speculation during the new moon.
- Those born between August 1st and August 7th will have better chances in speculation during the second quarter of the moon.
- Those born between August 8th and August 16th will have better chance in speculation during the full moon.
- Those born between August 17th and August 23rd will have better chances in speculation during the fourth quarter of the moon.
- NEARLY ALL CALENDARS GIVE THE FOUR QUARTERS OF THE MOON.

NUMEROLOGY

According to the science of Numerology the Celestial Number of Leo is 5. The Sun, the ruling planet of this sign, has 9 as its numerical value. Combining these two numbers we have 5 plus 9, which equals 14. This must be reduced to a simple digit, therefore, 1 plus 4 equals 5. The number 5 is the key number for all persons born in Leo. Bear this in mind on all occasions. When you buy a ticket of any sort, see that 5 is the predominating number, Room number 5 in a hotel, a street number containing a 5 or several 5's, horse number 5 in a race, player number 5 in a sport game, cards that total 5 in a card game, a 5 rolled with dice, 5 on a spin wheel, etc., are considered fortunate for you.

ILLUSTRATION : Suppose you have two cards in your hand, a two spot and a three-spot. Now, 2 plus 3 equals 5, therefore, such a hand would be fortunate for you or any other combination of cards that could be added and any other combination of cards that could be added and reduced to 5. If you should have a combination that totals 41, that would also reduce to 4; 4 plus 1 equals 5.

Use the same method with other combinations and totals.

FIND YOUR BEST DAYS FOR SPECULATION :

Any day of the month that totals 5 is considered fortunate for you, thus, the 14th or 23rd because these dates reduce to a single digit 5. Therefore, the days of the month that are best for speculation for you are the 5th, 14th and 23rd. However, you should engage in speculation only in your proper periods as explained below.

PROPER HOURS FOR SPECULATION :

The proper hour for speculation is when your ruling planet is governing. Refer to your daily paper, almanac or calendar to find the time of sunrise; then count the hours after sunrise. These hours are the same every week, month and year. Only the time of sunrise changes.

HOURS FOR SPECULATION : Sunday : 1st, 8th, 15th, 22nd, hour after sunrise. Monday : 5th, 12th, 19th hour after sunrise. Tuesday : 2nd, 9th, 16th, 23rd hour after sunrise. Wednesday : 6th, 13th, 20th hour after sunrise. Thursday : 3rd, 10th, 17th, 24th hour after sunrise. Friday : 7th, 14th, 21st hour after sunrise. Saturday : 4th, 11th, 18th hour after sunrise.

Activate North-West for new opportunities, foreign travel, gains from helpful people. Wear a Yellow/Golden bracelet, watch with a golden strap, put up a windchime in north-west and keep a yellow eight-angled pyramid in North-West.

LUCKY DAYS-VIRGO

FOR ALL THOSE BORN BETWEEN AUGUST 24TH TO SEPT. 23RD

ASTROLOGY indicates the exact periods when you should speculate and when you should not do so. The Earth going through the twelve signs of the Zodiac forms certain configuration which indicate your prospects in any game of chance. Thus your regular periods every year when you will win or when you may lose, and it is up to you to make use to this information. In order to make this reading the most accurate your sign has been divided into three sections. The division, by decanate, gives you about ten days which are influenced by the Sun's transits.

IF YOU ARE BORN BETWEEN AUGUST 24th to 31st and *SEPTEMBER* 1st to 3rd, you may speculate during the following periods and may expect to win :

April	21st	to	1st of May
June	22nd	to	2nd of July
October	24th	to	3rd of Nov.
December	22nd	to	31st of Dec.

From August 23rd to September 3rd, you will also be tempted to speculate, yet must determine for yourself whether or not you can win. Do not speculate from 1st of June and November 23rd to 3rd of December.

IF YOU ARE BORN BETWEEN SEPTEMBER 4th to 13th. You may speculate during the following periods and may expect to win :

January	1st	to	10th
May	2nd 1st	to	12th
July	3rd 2nd	to	13th
November	2nd 1st	to	12th

From September 3rd to 14th you will be tempted to speculate, yet must determine for yourself whether or not you can win. Do not speculate from March 1st to 11th, June 2nd to 12th and December 2nd to 13th.

IF YOU ARE BORN ON SEPTEMBER 14th, 15th, 16th, 17th, 18th, 19th, 20th, 21st and 22nd, you may speculate during the following periods and may expect to win :

January	11th	to	21st
May	11th	to	21st
July	12th	to	23rd
November	12th	to	22nd

From September 12th to 23rd, you will be tempted to speculate, yet must determine for yourself whether or not you can win. Do not speculate from March 9th to 20th, June 11th to 21st and December 12th to 22nd.

All Virgo-born are inclined to take chances from December 23rd to January 20th. When you speculate in cooperation with others, it would be advisable that your partner is born under one of the following signs :

Pisces	Feb. 20th	to	Mar. 20th
Taurus	Apr. 21st	to	May 21st
Cancer	June 22nd	to	July 23rd
Virgo	Aug. 24th	to	Sept. 23rd
Scorpio	Oct. 24th	to	Nov. 22nd
Capricorn	Dec. 23rd	to	Jan. 20th

IMPORTANT : **Read pages 64-67** for the cycles of

JUPITER, which indicate your fortunate years. When under an Adverse Cycle you are warned to be most careful in your speculations, as it is a period when you will not be very lucky.

SPECIAL TIPS

- Those born between August 24th and August 31st will have better chances in speculation during the new moon.
- Those born between September 1st and September 7th will have better chances of speculation during the second quarter of the moon.
- Those born between September 8th and September 17th will have better chances of speculation during the full moon.
- Those born between September 18th and September 23rd will have better chances in speculation during the fourth quarter of the moon.
- NEARLY ALL CALENDARS GIVE THE FOUR QUARTERS OF THE MOON.

NUMEROLOGY

According to the science of Numerology the Celestial Number of Virgo is 8. Mercury, the ruling planet of this sign has the numerical value of 4. Combining these two numbers we have 8 plus 4 which equals 12. This number must be reduced to a single digit, therefore : 1 plus 2 equals 3. Number 3 is the key number for all people born in Virgo. Bear this in mind on all occasions. When you buy a ticket of any sort, see that 3 is the predominating number, if it contains a serial number, Room number 3 in a hotel, a street number containing a 3 or several 3's, horse number 3 in a race, player number 3 in a sport game, cards that total 3 in a card game, a 3 rolled with dice, 3 on a spin wheel, etc., are considered fortunate for you.

ILLUSTRATION : Suppose you have two cards in your hand, a ten-spot and a two-spot. Now, 10 plus 2 equals 12 and reducing to a single digit, 1 plus 2 equals 3; therefore, such a hand would be fortunate for you. Any other combination of cards that could be added and reduced to 3 can also be used. If you should have a combination that equals 21, that would reduce to 2 etc. Use the same method with other combinations or totals.

FIND YOUR BEST DAYS FOR SPECULATION :

Any day of any month that totals 3 is considered fortunate for you, thus : 12th, 21st, 30th, because these dates reduce to the single digit 3. Therefore, the days of the month that are best for speculation for you are the 3rd, 12th, 21st, 30th. However, you should engage in speculation only in your proper periods as explained below.

PROPER HOURS FOR SPECULATION :

The proper hour for speculation is when your ruling planet is governing. Refer to your daily paper, almanac or calendar to find the time of sunrise, then count the hours after sunrise. These hours are the same every week, month and year. Only the time of sunrise changes.

HOURS FOR SPECULATION—Sunday : 3rd, 10th, 17th, 24th hour after sunrise. Monday : 7th, 14th, 21st hour after sunrise. Tuesday : 4th, 11th, 18th hour after sunrise. Tuesday : 4th, 8th, 15th, 22nd hour after sunrise. Friday : 2nd, 9th, 16th, 23rd hour after sunrise. Saturday : 6th, 13th, 20th hour after sunrise.

Do not have a toilet or a puja room or any article related to fire i.e. electric meter, inverter, empty/filled gas cylinders etc. under a staircase.

LUCKY DAYS—LIBRA

FOR ALL THOSE BORN BETWEEN SEPT. 24TH TO OCT. 23RD

ASTROLOGY indicates the exact periods when you should speculate and when you should not do so. The Earth going through the Twelve signs of the Zodiac forms certain configurations which indicate your prospects in any game of chance. Thus, you have regular periods every year when you will win or when you may lose, and it is up to you to make use of the information. In order to make this reading the most accurate your sign has been divided into three sections. This division, by decanate, gives you about ten days which are influenced by the Sun's transits.

IF YOU ARE BORN BETWEEN SEPTEMBER 24th to 30th and October 1st to 3rd, you may speculate during the following periods and may expect to win :

January	21st	to	30th
May	22nd	to	1st of June
July	24th	to	3rd of August
November	23rd	to	3rd of December

From September 23rd to October 5th you will also be tempted to speculate, yet must determine for yourself whether or not you can win. Do not speculate from March 21st to 31st, June 22nd to 3rd of July, and December 22nd to 31st.

IF YOU ARE BORN BETWEEN OCTOBER 4th to13th. You may speculate during the following periods and may expect to win :

January	31st	to	9th of Feb.
June	1st	to	12th
August	3rd	to	14th
December	2nd	to	12th

From October 2nd to 14th you will also be tempted to speculate, yet must determine for yourself whether or not you can win. Do not speculate from January 1st to 12th, April 1st to 11th, and July 2nd to 15th.

IF YOU ARE BORN BETWEEN OCTOBER 14th to 23rd you may speculate during the following periods and expect to win :

February	9th	to	19th
June	11th	to	21st
August	12th	to	23rd
December	11th	to	22nd

From October 10th to 23rd you will also be tempted to speculate, yet must determine for yourself whether or not you can win. Do not speculate from January 9th to 20th, April 19th to 20th and July 12th to 23rd.

All Libra-born are inclined to take chances between January 21st and February 19th. When you speculate in cooperation with others, it would be advisable that your partner is born under one of the following signs :

Aquarius	Jan. 21st	to	Feb. 19th
Aries	Mar. 21st	to	Apr. 20th
Geminin	May 22nd	to	June 21st
Leo	July 24th	to	Aug. 23rd
Libra	Sept. 24th	to	Oct. 23rd
Sagittarius	Nov 23rd	to	Dec. 22nd

IMPORTANT—**Read pages 64-67** for the cycle of JUPITER which indicates your fortunate years. When under an Adverse Cycle you are warned to be most careful in your speculations, as it is a period when you will not be very lucky.

SPECIAL TIPS

- Those born between September 24th and September 30th will have better chances in speculation during the new moon.
- Those born between October 1st and October 17th will have better chances in speculation during the second quarter of the moon.
- Those born between October 8th and October 17th will have better chances in speculation during the full moon.
- Those born between October 18th and October 23rd will have better chances in speculation during the fourth quarter of the moon.
- NEARLY ALL CALENDARS GIVE THE FOUR QUARTERS OF THE MOON.

NUMEROLOGY

According to the science of Numerology, the celestial number of libra is 6. Venus, the ruling planet of this sign, has a numerical value of 9. Combining these two numbers we have 6 plus 9 which equal 15. This number must be reduced to a single digit, therefore : 1 plus 5 equals 6. The number 6 is the key number of all persons born under Libra. Bear this in mind at all times. When you buy a ticket of any sort see that the serial number has 6 as the predominating number. Room number 6 in a hotel, a street number containing a 6 or several 6's, horse number 6 in a race, player number 6 in a sport game, cards that total 6 in a card game, a 6 rolled with dice, 6 on a spin wheel, etc., are considered fortunate for you.

ILLUSTRATION : Suppose you have two cards in your hand: a four-spot and a two-spot. Now, 4 plus 2 equals 6 therefore such a hand would be fortunate for you or any other combination that totals and reduces to 6. If you should have a combination that total 51, that would reduce to 6 etc. Use the same method with other combinations and totals.

FIND YOUR BEST DAYS FOR SPECULATION :

Any day of the month that totals 6 is considered fortunate for you, thus : 5th, 24th : because these dates reduce to the single digit 6. Therefore the days of the month that are best for speculations for you are : 6th, 15th, 24th. However, you should engage in speculation only in your proper periods as explained below.

PROPER HOURS FOR SPECULATION :

The proper hour for speculation is when your ruling planet is governing. Refer to your daily paper, almanac or calendar to find the time of sunrise, then count the hours after sunrise. These hours are the same every week, month and year. Only the time of sunrise changes.

HOURS FOR SPECULATION—Sunday : 2nd, 9th, 16th, 23rd hour after sunrise. Monday : 6th, 13th, 20th hour after sunrise. Tuesday : 3rd, 8th, 15th, 24th hour after sunrise. Wednesday : 7th, 14th, 21st hour after sunrise. Thursday : 4th, 11th, 18th hour after sunrise. Friday : 1st, 8th, 15th, 22nd hour after sunrise. Saturday : 5th, 12th, 19th hour after sunrise.

LUCKY DAYS—SCORPIO

FOR ALL THOSE BORN BETWEEN OCT. 24TH TO NOVEMBER 22ND

ASTROLOGY indicates the exact periods when you should speculate and when you should not do so. The Earth going through the Twelve signs of the Zodiac forms certain configurations which indicate your prospects in any game of chance. Thus, you have regular periods every year when you will win or when you may lose, and it is up to you to make use of this information. In order to make this reading the most accurate your sign has been divided into three sections. This division, by decanate, gives you about ten days which are influenced by the Sun's transits.

IF YOU ARE BORN ON OCTOBER 24th, 25th, 26th, 27th, 28th, 29th, 30th, 31st & NOVEMBER 1st, 2nd you may speculate during the following periods and may expect to win :

February	20th	to	29th
June	22nd	to	2nd of July
August	24th	to	3rd of Sept.
December	21st	to	31st

From October 23rd to November 3rd, you will also be tempted to speculate, yet must determine for yourself whether you can win. Do not speculate from January 20th to 31st, April 21st to 2nd of May, and July 23rd to 4th of August.

IF YOU ARE BORN BETWEEN NOVEMBER 3rd to 12th

you may speculate during the following periods and may expect to win :

January	1st	to	11th
March	1st	to	10th
July	2nd	to	13th
September	3rd	to	14th

From November 1st to 13th you will also be tempted to speculate, yet must determine for yourself whether you can win. Do not speculate from February 1st to 12th, May 1st to 12th and August 2nd to 15th.

IF YOU ARE BORN BETWEEN NOVEMBER 13th to 22nd you may speculate during the following periods and expect to win :

February	20th	to	29th
June	22nd	to	2nd of July
August	24th	to	3rd of Sept.
December	21st	to	31st

From October 23rd to November 3rd you will also be tempted to speculate, yet must determine for yourself whether you can win. Do not speculate from January 20th to 31st, April 21st to 2nd of May, and July 23rd to 4th of August.

IF YOU ARE BORN BETWEEN NOVEMBER 3rd to12th you may speculate during the following periods and may expect to win :

January	1st	to	11th
March	1st	to	10th
July	2nd	to	13th
September	3rd	to	14th

From November 1st to 13th you will also be tempted to speculate, yet must determine for yourself whether you can win. Do not speculate from February 1st to 12th, May 1st to 12th and August 2nd to 15th.

IF YOU ARE BORN BETWEEN NOVEMBER 13th to 22nd you may speculate during the following periods and expect to win :

January	11th	to	20th
March	10th	to	20th
July	12th	to	23rd
September	13th	to	23rd

From November 10th to 23rd you will also be tempted to speculate, yet must determine for yourself whether you can win. Do not speculate from February 8th to 20th, May 11th to 21st, and August 13th to 23rd.

All Scorpio-born are inclined to take chances from February 20th to March 20th. When you speculate in cooperation with others, it would be advisable that your partner is born under one of the following signs :

Capricorn	Dec. 23rd	to	Jan 20th
Pisces	Feb. 20th	to	March 20th
Taurus	Apr. 21st	to	May 21st
Cancer	June 22nd	to	July 23rd
Virgo	Aug. 24th	to	Sept. 23rd
Scorpio	Oct. 24th	to	Nov. 22nd

IMPORTANT : **Read page 64-67** for the cycle of JUPITER which indicates your fortunate years. When under an Adverse Cycle you are warned to be most careful in you speculation, as it is a period when you will not be very lucky.

SPECIAL TIPS

- Those born between October 24th and October 30th will have better chances in speculation during the new moon.
- Those born between October 31st and November 8th will have better chance in speculation during the second quarter of the moon.

- Those born between November 9th and November 16th will have better chances in speculation during the full moon.
- Those born between November 17th and November 22nd will have better chances in speculation during the fourth quarter of the moon.
- NEARLY ALL CALENDARS GIVE THE FOUR QUARTERS OF THE MOON.

NUMEROLOGY

According to the science of numerology, the celestial number of Scorpio is 5. Pluto, the ruling planet of this sign has the numerical value of 3. Combining these two numbers we have : 5 plus 3 equals 8. Number 8 is the key number for all persons born in Scorpio. Bear this in mind on all occasions. When you buy a ticket of any sort, see that the serial number has 8 as the predominating number, Room number 8 in hotel, a street number containing an 8 or several 8's, horse number 8 in a race, player number 8 in a sport game, cards that totals 8 in a card game, an 8 rolled with dice, 8 on a spin wheel, etc. are considered fortunate for you.

ILLUSTRATION : Suppose you have two cards in your hand : a four spot and another four spot. Now 4 plus 4 equals 8. Therefore such a hand would be fortunate for you, or any other combination of cards that would totals 8. If you have a combination that totals 26 or 53, that would also total 8, Use the same methods with other combination and totals.

FIND YOUR BEST DAYS FOR SPECULATION :

Any day of any month that totals 8 is considered fortunate for you, thus; 17th and 26th, because these days reduce to the single digit 8. Therefore, the best days for speculation for you are : 8th, 17th, and 26th. However, you should engage in speculation only in your proper periods as explained below.

PROPER HOURS FOR SPECULATION :

The proper hour for speculation is when your ruling planet is governing. Refer to your daily paper, almanac or calender to find the time of sunrise; then count the hours after sunrise. These hours are the same every week, month and year. Only the time of sunrise changes.

HOURS FOR SPECULATION : Sunday : 7th, 14th, 21st hour after sunrise. Monday : 4th, 11th, 18th hour after sunrise, Tuesday : 1st, 8th, 11th, 22nd hour after sunrise, Wednesday : 5th, 12th, 19th hour after sunrise. Thursday : 2nd, 9th, 16th, 23rd hour sunrise. Friday : 6th, 13th, 20th hour after sunrise. Saturday : 3rd, 10th, 17th. 24th hour after sunrise.

LUCKY DAYS—SAGITTARIUS

FOR ALL THOSE BORN BETWEEN NOVEMBER 23RD TO DEC. 22ND

ASTROLOGY indicates the exact periods when you should speculate and when you should not do so. The Earth going through the Twelve signs of the Zodiac forms certain configurations which indicate your prospects in any game of chance. Thus, you have regular periods every year when you will win or when you may lose, and it is up to you to make use of this information. In order to make this reading the most accurate your sign has been divided into three sections. The division, by decanate, gives you about ten days which are influenced by the Sun's transits.

IF YOU ARE BORN BETWEEN NOVEMBER 23rd to 30th & DECEMBER 1st, 2nd you may speculate during the following periods and expect to win :

January	21st	to	30th
March	21st	to	31st
July	23rd	to	3rd of August
September	23rd	to	4th of October.

IF YOU ARE BORN BETWEEN DECEMBER 3rd to 12th you may speculate during the following periods and may expect to win :

January	31st	to	9th of February
April	1st	to	11th

August	12	th	of 23rd
October	3rd	to	14th.

From December 1st to 14th, you will also be tempted to speculate, you must determine for yourself whether or not you can win. Do not speculate from March 1st to 13th, June 1st to 12th, and September 2nd to 14th.

IF YOU ARE BORN BETWEEN DECEMBER 13th to 22nd you may speculate during the following periods and expect to win :

February	9th	to	20th
April	10th	to	20th
August	13th	to	23rd
October	12th	to	23rd

From December 10th to 22nd you will also be tempted to speculate, yet must determine for yourself whether or not you can win. Do not speculate from March 10th to 21st, June 11st to 21st, and September 12th to 23rd.

All Sagittarius-born are inclined to take chances between March 21st to April 20th. When you speculate in cooperation with others, it would be advisable that your partner is born under one of the following signs :

Aquarius	Jan. 21st	to	Feb. 19th
Aries	Mar. 21st	to	Apr. 20th
Gemini	May 22nd	to	June 21st
Leo	July 24th	to	Aug. 23rd
Libra	Sept. 24th	to	Oct. 23rd
Sagittarius	Nov. 23rd	to	Dec. 22nd.

IMPORTANT : **Read page 64-67** for the cycle of JUPITER which indicates your fortunate years. When under an Adverse Cycle you are warned to be most careful in your speculations, as it is a period when you will not be every lucky.

SPECIAL TIPS

- Those born between November 23rd and November 29th will have better chances in speculation during the new moon.
- Those born between November 30th and December 7th will have better chances in speculation during the second quarter of the moon.
- Those born between December 8th and December 16th will have better chances in speculation during the full moon.
- Those born between December 17th and December 22nd will have better chances in speculation during the fourth quarter of the moon.
- NEARLY ALL CALENDARS GIVE THE FOUR QUARTERS OF THE MOON.

NUMEROLOGY

According to the science of numerology, the celestial number of Sagittarius is 8. Jupiter, the ruling planet of this sign, has the numerical valve of 9. Combining these two numbers we have : 8 plus 9 equals 17. Now this must be reduced to a single digit, thus : 1 plus 7 equals 8. The key number for all persons born in Sagittarius is 8, the same as for Scorpio. There are only 9 digits, therefore some Zodiacal signs have duplicate numbers since there are 12 signs. Bear in mind at all times that 8 is your celestial number. When you buy a ticket of any sort, see that the serial number 8 in a hotel, player number 8 in a sport games, horse number 8 in a race, a street number with an 8 or several 8's, cards that total 8 in a card game, an 8 rolled with dice, 8 in a spin wheel, etc. are considered fortunate for you.

ILLUSTRATION : Suppose you have two cards in your hand: a six-spot a two-spot. Now 6 plus 2 equals 8, therefore such a hand would be fortunate for you, or any other combination of cards that would total 8. If you have a combination of cards that would total 8. If you have a combination that totals 35 or 53, that would also reduce to 8. Use the same method for other combinations.

FIND YOUR BEST DAYS FOR SPECULATION :

Any day of any month that totals 8 is considered fortunate for you, thus; 17th and 26th. However, you should engage in speculation only in your proper periods as explained below.

PROPER HOURS FOR SPECULATION :

The proper hour for speculation is when your ruling planet is governing. Refer to you daily paper, almanac or calendar to find the time to sunrise. Then count the hours after sunrise. These hours are the same every week, month, and year. Only the time of sunrise changes.

HOURS FOR SPECULATION : Sunday : 6th, 13th, 20th hour after sunrise. Monday : 3rd, 10th, 17th, 24th hour after sunrise. Tuesday : 7th, 14th, 21st hour after sunrise. Wednesday : 4th, 11th, 18th, hour after sunrise. Thursday : 1st 8th, 15th, 22nd hour after sunrise. Friday : 5th, 12th, 19th hour after sunrise. Saturday : 2nd, 9th, 16th, 23rd hour after sunrise.

LUCKY DAYS—CAPRICORN

FOR ALL THOSE BORN BETWEEN DEC. 23RD TO JAN 20TH

ASTROLOGY indicates the exact periods when you should speculate and when you should not do so. The Earth going through the Twelve signs of the Zodiac forms certain configurations which indicate your prospects in any game of chance. Thus, you have regular periods every year when you will win or when you may lose, and it is up to you to make use of this information. In order to make this reading the most accurate your sign has been divided into three sections. This division, by decanate, gives you about ten days which are influenced by the Sun's transits.

IF YOU ARE BORN BETWEEN DECEMBER 22nd to 31st you may speculate during the following periods and may expect to win:

February	20th	to	29th
April	21st	to	2nd of May
August	23rd	to	3rd of Sept.
October	22nd	to	2nd of Nov.

From December 20th to 31st you will also be tempted to speculate, yet must determine for yourself whether you can win. Do not speculate from March 21st to 31st, June 22nd to 3rd of July, and September 24th to 4th of October.

IF YOU ARE BORN BETWEEN JANUARY 1st to 10th you

may speculate during the following periods and expect to win :

March	1st	to	10th
May	2nd	to	12th
September	4th	to	14th
November	2nd	to	13th

From January 1st to 12th you will also be tempted to speculate, yet must determine for yourself whether or not you can win. Do not speculate from April 1st to 11th, July 2nd to 13th, and October 3rd to 14.

IF YOU ARE BORN BETWEEN JANUARY 11th to 20th you may speculate during the following periods and expect to win :

March	10th	to	20th
May	11th	to	21st
September	13th	to	24th
November	13th	to	22nd

From January 9th to 21st you will also be tempted to speculate, yet must determine for yourself whether or not you can win. Do not speculate from April 10th to 20th, July 13th to 23rd, and October 12th to 23rd.

All Capricorn-born are inclined to take chances between April 21st to May 21st. When you speculate in cooperation with others, it would be advisable that your partner is born under one of the following signs :

Capricorn	Dec. 23rd	to	Jan. 20th
Pisces	Feb. 20th	to	Mar. 20th
Taurus	Apr. 21st	to	May 21st
Cancer	June 22nd	to	July 23rd
Virgo	Aug. 24th	to	Sept. 23rd
Scorpio	Oct. 24th	to	Nov. 22nd

IMPORTANT : **Read pages 64-67** for the Cycle of Jupiter, which indicate your fortunate years. When under an adverse Cycle, you are warned to be most careful in your speculation, as it is a period when you will not be very lucky.

SPECIAL TIPS

- Those born between December 23rd to December 30th will have better chances in speculation during the new moon.
- Those born between December 31st and January 6th will have better chances in speculation during the second quarter of the moon.
- Those born between January 7th and January 13th will have better chances in speculation during the full moon.
- Those born between January 15th to January 20th will have better chances in speculating during the fourth quarters of moon.

NUMEROLOGY

According to the science of numerology, the celestial number of Carpricorn is 8. Saturn, the ruling planet of this sign, has the numerical value of 3. Combining those number we have : 8 plus 3 which equal 11. This must be reduced to a single digit, thus : 1 plus 1 equals 2. The key number for all persons born in Capricorn is 2, the same as for those born in Cancer. There are only nine digits, therefore signs have duplicate numbers since there are only 12 signs. Bear in mind at all times that 2 is your celestial number. When you buy a ticket of any sort, see that the serial number has 2 predominating, room number 2 in a hotel, player number 2 in a sport game, horse number 2 in a race, a street number with 2 or several 2's in it, card game, a 2 rolled with dice, 2 on a spin wheel, etc. are considered fortunate for you.

ILLUSTRATION : Suppose you have two cards in your hand: a ten-spot and an ace. Now 10 plus 1 equal 11 and that reduced to a single digit equals 2, therefore, such a hand would be fortunate for you, or any other combination of cards that totals 2. If you have a combination that totals 20, that will also reduce to 2. Use the same method for other combinations.

FIND YOUR BEST DAYS FOR SPECULATION :

Any days of any month that totals 2 is considered fortunate for you, thus : 11th, 29th, etc., because these reduce to the single digit 2. Therefore, the best days for speculation for you are 2nd, 11th and 29th. However, you should speculate only in your proper periods as explained below :

PROPER HOURS FOR SPECULATION :

The proper hour for speculation is when your ruling planet is governing. Refer to your daily paper, almanac of calender to find the time of sunrise, then count the hours after sunrise. These hours are the same every week, month and year. Only the time of sunrise changes.

HOURS FOR SPECULATION : Sunday : 5th, 12th, 19th hours after sunrise. Monday : 2nd, 9th, 23rd hour after sunrise. Tuesday : 6th, 13th, 20th hour after sunrise. Wednesday : 3rd, 8th, 15th, 24th hour after sunrise. Thursday : 7th, 14th, 21st hour after sunrise. Friday : 4th, 11th, 18th hour after sunrise. Saturday : 1st, 10th, 17th, 22nd hour after sunrise.

Control South-West(confusion, indecision & obstacles in life) by keeping a picture/ Painting of high peak mountains without water. Wear a silica pendant/necklace/ bracelet for more strength and stability.

LUCKY DAYS—AQUARIUS

FOR ALL THOSE BORN BETWEEN JAN. 21ST TO FEB. 19TH

ASTROLOGY indicates the exact periods when you should speculate and when you should not do so. This Earth going through the twelve signs of the Zodiac forms certain configurations which indicate your prospects in any game of chance. Thus you have regular periods every year when you will win or when you may lose, and it is up to you to make this reading the most accurate. Your sign has been divided into three sections. This division, by decanate, gives you about ten days which are influenced by the sun's transits.

IF YOU ARE BORN BETWEEN JANUARY 21st to 30th you may speculate during the following periods and may expect to win:

March	21st	to	31st
May	22nd	to	2nd of June

From January 20th to 31st you will also be tempted to speculate, yet must determine for yourself whether or not you can win. Do not speculate from April 21st to 2nd of May, July 23rd to 3rd of August, and October 24th to 3rd of November.

IF YOU ARE BORN BETWEEN JANUARY 31st and FEBRUARY 1st to 9th you may speculate during the following periods and expect to win :

April	3rd	to	12th
June	3rd	to	11th
October	1st	to	13th
December	1st	to	13th

From January 30th to February 10th you will also be tempted to speculate, yet you must determine for yourself whether or not you can win. Do not speculate from May 2nd to 12 th, August 2nd to 14th, and November 1st to 12th.

IF YOU ARE BORN BETWEEN FEBRUARY 10th to 19th you may speculate during the following periods and expect to win :

April	11th	to	20th
June	11th	to	21st
October	13th	to	23rd
December	11th	to	22nd

From February 9th to 20th you will also be tempted to speculate, yet must determine for yourself whether or not you can win. Do not speculate from May 10th to 22nd, August 13th to 23rd, and November 11th to 22nd.

All Aquarius-born are inclined to take chances between May 22nd and June 21st. When you speculate in cooperation with others, it would be advisable that your partner is born under one of the following signs :

Aries	Mar. 21st	to	Apr. 20th
Gemini	May 22nd	to	June 21st
Aquarius	Jan. 21st	to	Fen. 19th
Leo	July 24th	to	Aug. 23rd
Libra	Sept. 24th	to	Oct. 23rd
Sagittarius	Nov. 23rd	to	Dec. 22nd

IMPORTANT : **Read pages 64-67** for the Cycle of Jupiter, which indicate your fortunate years. When under an adverse Cycle, you are warned to be most careful in your speculation, as it is a period when you will not be very lucky.

SPECIAL TIPS

- Those born between January 21st and January 28th will have better chances in speculation during the new moon.
- Those born between January 29th and February 6th will have better chances in speculation during the second quarter of the moon.
- Those born between February 7th and February 14th will have better chances in speculation during the full moon.
- Those born between February 15th and February 19th will have better chances in speculation during the fourth quarter of the moon.

NUMEROLOGY

According to the science of Numerology the celestial number of Aquarius is 8. Uranus, the ruling planet of this sign, has the numerical value of 4. Combining these two numbers we have : 8 plus 4 which equals 12. This must be reduced to a single digit, Thus : 1 plus 2 equals 3. The key number of all person born in Aquarius is 3, the same as Virgo. There are only 9 digits, therefore some signs must have duplicate numbers since there are 12 signs. Bear in mind at all times that 3 is your celestial number. When you buy a ticket of any sort see that the serial number has 3 or several 3's, horse number 3 in a race, player number 3 in a sport game, cards that total 3 in a card game, a 3 rolled with dice, 3 on a spin wheel, etc., are considered fortunate for you.

ILLUSTRATION : Suppose you have two cards in your hand : a nine-spot and a three-spot. Now, 9 plus 3 equals 12 and that reduced to a single digit equal 3, therefore such a hand would be fortunate for you, or any other combination of cards that would total 3. If you have a combination that totals 48 or 66, that would total 12 and this then reduced to single digit gives 3. Use the same method with other combinations and totals.

FIND YOUR BEST DAYS FOR SPECULATION :

Any day of any month that totals 3 is considered fortunate for you, thus : 12th, 21st, 30th because these reduce to the single digit 3. Therefore, the best days for speculation for you are 3rd, 12th, 21st and 30th. However, you should speculate only in your proper periods as explained below.

PROPER HOURS FOR SPECULATION :

The proper hour for speculation is when your ruling planet is governing. Refer to your daily paper, almanac or calendar to find the time of sunrise, then count the time of sunrise, then count the hours after sunrise. These hours are the same every week, month and year. Only the time of sunrise changes.

HOURS FOR SPECULATION : Sunday : 3rd, 10th, 17th, 24th hour after sunrise, Monday : 7th, 14th, 21st hour after sunrise. Tuesday : 4th, 11th, 18th hour after sunrise. Wednesday : 5th, 12th, 19th hour after sunrise. Thursday : 2nd, 9th, 16th, 23rd hour after sunrise. Friday : 6th, 13th, 20th hour after sunrise. Saturday : 1st, 8th, 15th, 22nd hour after sunrise.

For harmonious life do not hang a painting/picture or idol depicting war, crime, agony or distress in your office/ residence/work-place.

LUCKY DAYS—PISCES

FOR ALL THOSE BORN BETWEEN FEB. 20TH TO MAR. 20TH

ASTROLOGY indicates the exact period when you should speculate and when you should not do so. The earth going through the twelve signs of the Zodiac forms certain configuration which indicate your prospects in any game of chance. Thus you have regular periods every year when you will win or when you may lose, and it is up to you to make use of this information. In order to make this reading the most accurate, your sign has been divided into three sections. This division, by decanate, gives you about ten days which are influenced by the Sun's transits.

IF YOU ARE BORN BETWEEN FEBRUARY 20th to 29th. You may speculate during the following periods and expect to win :

April	21st	to	2nd of May
June	22nd	to	3rd of July
October	23rd	to	2nd of Nov.
December	22nd	to	31st

From February 19th to 29th you will also be tempted to speculate, yet must determine for yourself whether or not you can win. Do not speculate from May 21st to 2nd of June, August 23rd to 4th of September, and November 21st to 4th of December.

IF YOU ARE BORN BETWEEN MARCH 1st to 11th you may speculate during the following periods and expect to win :

January	1st	to	10th
May	1st	to	12th
July	2nd	to	13th
November	1st	to	12th

From March 1st 12th you will also be tempted to speculate, yet must determine for yourself whether or not you can win. Do not speculate from June 1st to 13th, September 2nd to 13th, and December 1st to 12th.

IF YOU ARE BORN BETWEEN MARCH 11th to 20th you may speculate during the following periods and expect to win :

January	10th	to	20th
May	11th	to	21st
July	13th	to	23rd
November	11th	to	22nd

From March 9th to 21st you will also be tempted to speculate, yet must determine for yourself whether or not you can win. Do not speculate from June 10th to 22nd.

All Pisces-born are inclined to take chances between June 22nd and July 23rd. When you speculate in cooperation with others, it would be advisable that your partner is born under one of the following signs :

Capricorn	Dec. 23rd	to	Jan. 20th
Pisces	Feb. 20th	to	Mar. 20th
Taurus	Apr. 21st	to	May 21st
Cancer	June 22nd	to	July 23rd
Virgo	Aug. 24th	to	Sept. 23rd
Scorpio	Oct. 24th	to	Nov. 22nd

IMPORTANT : **Read pages 64-67** for the Cycle of Jupiter, which indicate your fortunate years. When under an adverse Cycle, you are warned to be most careful in your speculation, as it is a period when you will not be very lucky.

SPECIAL TIPS

- Those born between February 20th and February 26th will have better chances in speculation during the new moon.
- Those born between February 27th and March 5th will have better chances in speculation during the second quarter of the moon.
- Those born between March 6th and March 13th will have better chances in speculations during the full moon.
- Those born between March 14th and March 20th will have better chances in speculation during the fourth quarter of the moon.
- NEARLY ALL CALENDARS GIVE THE FOUR QUARTERS OF THE MOON.

NUMEROLOGY

According to the science of Numerology the celestial number of Pisces is 8. Neptune, the ruling planet of this sign, has the numerical value of 5. Combining these two numbers we have : 8 plus 5 equals 13. This must be reduced to a single digit, thus : 1 plus 3 equals 4. Number 4 is the key number for all persons born in Pisces, the same as for those born in Aries. There are only nine digits, therefore some signs will have duplicate numbers since there are 12 signs. Bear in mind that your key number is 4. When you buy a ticket of any sort, see that the serial number 4 is the predominating number. Room number 4 in a hotel, street number containing 4 or several 4's, horse number 4 in a race, player number 4 in a sport game, cards that total 4 in a card game, a 4 rolled with dice, 4 on a spin wheel, etc., are considered fortunate for you.

ILLUSTRATION : Suppose you have two cards in your hand : a nine-spot and a four-spot. Now, 9 plus 4 equals 13, and this when reduced equals 4, so this would be a fortunate hand for you, or any other combination that would be reduced to 4, etc. Use the same method with other combinations, such as 31st or 67 which reduce to 4.

FIND YOUR BEST DAYS FOR SPECULATION :

Any day of the month that totals 4 is considered fortunate for you, thus : 13th, 22nd and the 31st of a month, because these days reduce to a single digit, making 4. The days of the month that are best for speculation are : 4th, 13th, 22nd and 31st. However, you should engage in speculation only in your proper period as explained below.

PROPER HOURS FOR SPECULATION :

The proper hour for speculation is when your ruling planet in governing. Refer to you daily paper, almanac, or calendar to find the time of sunrise, then count the hours after sunrise. These hours are the same every week, month and year. Only the time of sunrise changes.

HOURS FOR SPECULATION : Sunday : 2nd, 9th, 16th, 23rd hour after sunrise. Monday 5th, 12th, 19th hour after sunrise. Tuesday : 6th, 13th, 20th hour after sunrise. Wednesday : 3rd, 10th, 17th, 24th hour after sunrise. Thursday : 7th, 14th, 21st hour after sunrise. Friday : 1st, 8th, 15th, 22nd hours after sunrise. Saturday : 4th, 11th, 18th hour after sunrise.

LUCKY DAYS

JUPITER, the largest planet in our solar system, plays an important role in our life. Infact its size is three times as big as all the rest of the planets put together. It takes twelve years for the planet to go through the twelve signs of the Zodiac and during this period it influences all human beings, and just as its power is so great as to change the course of comets, so does its influence change the destiny of empires and men. Its cycle is, therefore, 12 years; in other same place in the Heavens as at your birth and marks then the beginning of a new cycle for you. This law holds true for every man and woman, and thus it is possible to calculate the fortunate years for each one of us as well as to indicate those years when we are wasteful, extravagant and careless and thus face losses. The following interpretation of the Jupiter cycle is the same for all of us, yet this does not mean that it is general; for this planet takes one year to go through one sign and therefore its easy to calculate exactly its position for every year of your life.

King Bharthari said " To everything there is a season and a time for every purpose under the Heaven." This means that human life should be planned in accordance with the planetary influence operating at our birth and those influencing us now. But to each one of us is given the freedom to work in harmony with those great natural Laws or to act contrary to them. It is up to us to plan our lives in such a way that we expand under favorable influences and to hold back when the planets are at critical angles. Those that do not understand those laws go blindly ahead and blame destiny for their ill-luck. All of us, regardless of when born, have periods when we are fortunate and success smiles upon us, but from time to time, we are under a cycle when our affairs go wrong and opportunities are few. Lucky for us, those cycles come at regular intervals and thus it is possible to indicate exactly the cycle you are under at a certain air of your life.

Regardless of other planetary influences operating in your life, the following cycles are fortunate for you and it is up to you to make use of them :

FORTUNATE CYCLES : At the age of 16, 20, 22, 26, 28, 32, 38, 40, 44, 46, 50, 56, 58, 62, 64, 68, 70, 74, 76 and 80. Of course, you may have some difficulties those years but some good fortune will come your way, somebody will help you, an opportunity will present itself, and chances for making money are good. To those out of work it means that they will be able to find employment, even if it is not what they would like to have. Changes made will prove profitable and business will increase. It marks a fortunate time for expanding in business, to take long journeys, for legal affairs or to establish yourself securely. It is a time when things come our way, when we receive many gifts, when we win at games of chance or when the opposite sex favours us. Your fortunate cycles last about nine months and start about four months before your birth-month to four months afterwards. For many of us those are the prosperity years of our life.

Next for you to consider are the adverse cycles also called cycles of restrictions. They mark periods in your life when you will not feel well, when your blood will be impure and when you will be careless and extravagant. It is an adverse time to speculate or gamble and those in business should not expand nor take on anything new without being sure it not a wild scheme that will end up in law suit. Others will refuse to cooperate, and some of us may even lose our jobs and it would be foolish for you to take chances. Thus, you will protect yourself against illusion and disappointments.

Those cycles of restriction also operate for nine months, in fact, you will feel them about 4 months before your birth-month and the 4th month afterwards.

ADVERSE CYCLE : At the age of 15, 18, 21, 27, 30, 33, 39, 42, 45, 51, 54, 57, 63, 66, 69, 75, 78, 81. A new cycle starts about every twelve years of your life and marks a complete change in your affairs. No doubt you know that the world conditions are influenced by the Sun spots, whose cycle is about eleven and half years, therefore similar to your own cycle. Now it is not possible to tell you here without consulting the planets on the day and year you were born, whether you will have success or misfortune when such a cycle begins. Perhaps if you go back in your life and go over the events that took place at the age of 12 and 24, you can tell if the beginning of a new cycle is good or bad for you. New cycles starts for everybody at the age of 12, 24, 36, 48, 60, 72, 84, 96.

History records many amazing predictions about the destiny of nations, rulers and individuals, all based on cycles and this was the secret of the Egyptians as well as all past civilizations. It is up to everyone of us to make use of those cycles in our affairs. Before anyone should make a plan for the future, he should see if he is under a fortunate cycle or an adverse cycle. If it is a fortunate cycle, then he can go ahead with his plans to expand, take chances and make radical changes in his affairs; yet if the cycle is adverse, it means that he must wait for at least one more year before launching new ventures or making any radical changes.

There are, of course, other cycles yet we cannot go into them any further until you have learned to apply what you have just read. It would be very interesting for you to look back into your past and see how many fortunate happenings you can trace to the Fortunate Cycles and how many losses or sorrows you can show for the Adverse Cycles. Thus, you will learn one of the fundamental laws of life.

By giving you this information, it is hoped that you will be more successful and find greater happiness, also protect you and warn you against pifalls and losses. Nothing can be of greater value than to know whether you are lucky now or whether you must be or your guard. Just realize how may times Fate was kind to you and you did not take the opportunity. When your affairs are going smoothly and success is yours and you know that it is a Fortunate Cycle, you can time its end and thus do not expect your luck to last longer than it really will. If you are having success now and in a few months you will come under a critical cycle, then prepare yourself for it and do not live or act like your good fortune would keep on going on for many more months; Establish yourself and enjoy the good things that come your way. But if Fate is unkind to you, when every hope is gone, you will want to know just when luck, success and happiness will be your nest favorable cycles and when will come and then go. Prepare yourself for your ship to come in. Perhaps it would be good for you to ponder over the words of Cheiro, the Great– **"The lucky have whole days, and those they choose. The unlucky have but hours, and those they lose."**

POWER OF NUMBERS

There are many systems of character analysis and methods of making predictions but none perhaps as interesting as Numerology, since anyone may work it out. No long hours of tedious study are required. There are only a few simple rules to follow.

The Egyptians, the Greeks, the Arabians had systems of arriving at number vibrations, which are remarkably accurate. The teachings of the adepts in Numerology have come down to us from the remotest antiquity.

All letters have numerical equations; therefore all combinations of letters in names respond to a certain numerical value. When a name is given to a person, a city, book or anything, it immediately lets loose a certain occult force expressed in numbers. Nature in its most primitive of snow flakes, of growing plant cells, the mathematical precision of numbers. Note the geometric formation of snow flakes, of growing plant cells, the mathematical precision of the sunrise, the movements of the heavenly bodies, the procession of the seasons, etc. These, and other geometric or mathematical formulae, respond to various number values. In everyday life we answer to the numbers of our names, our birth, our locations by our reaction to certain things. Some names appeal to us immediately; others we pass by unnoticed. It is our reaction to the numerical magnetism which causes us either to ignore or notice them. The universe is operated with exact mathematical precision calculated to a fraction of a second.

Every expression of rhythm responds to a numerical measure to time. When you listen to music that thrills you, you are unconsciously harmonizing with certain number influences in the notes of the music; or when you dislike certain types of music, it is because the numerical value of such music is not in sympathy with your own name and birth numbers. Every day of life brings some good or adverse reaction to the magnetic influence of the numbers around you. They are in everything you see, hear or feel. It is impossible to escape them. The sooner you learn the value of these numbers the better you will be able to harmonize with life and people around you.

On the following pages the author gives a very simple system of number calculation so that you may become familiar with the influences in your daily life and get the best out of your newly acquired knowledge. This is the best out of your newly acquired knowledge. This is the system taught by the Egyptians, which is not complicated as other systems, such as the Chiness, the Greek and others.

THE ALPHABET

In any system of Numerology the letters of the alphabet respond to the 9 digits or single numbers. Numbers of two figures are not retained except in the cases of 11 and 22, which will be explained later. The letter of the alphabet must be reduced to single numbers; consequently more than one letter responds to the same number as shown below :

1	2	3	4	5	6	7	8	9
A	B	C	D	E	F	G	H	I
J	K	L	M	N	O	P	Q	R
S	T	U	V	W	X	Y	Z	

You will notice that the letters A, J and S have the numerical value of the number 1, while B, K and T have the value of 2, etc. Whatever number a letter is under, that is its numerical power or number vibration.

EXAMPLE OF NUMBERING A NAME

M..........4	S........1
A 1	M.......4
R............9	I........9
Y............7	T.......2
	H......8
21	24

We are now ready to begin transferring names into numbers. We will choose a simple name as an example. Preferably the first name and last name of a person should be written vertically, as it is easier to add this way than horizontally. We choose the name Asha Singh.

The name Mary responds to 21 and the name Smith responds to 24. To secure the full name vibration, it is necessary to add 21 plus 24, which equals 45. This is a double number, so we will add 4 plus 5, which equals 9. This young lady then responds to the name number of 9. You may now refer to the indications of the number in the following pages and find out what the number 9 denotes.

We will now suppose that Asha Singh's birth-date is June 8, 1912. To transfer this into numerical value, we would write it thus : 6-8-1912, because June is the sixth month. Now add these numbers together : 6 plus 8, plus 1, Plus 9, plus 1, plus 2, equals 27. This totals is a double number so we add 2 plus 7, which equals 9. We find that Asha Singh's birthdate is 9, the same as her name number. Any number derived from the birthdate is called the Birth Path. Now we wish to find her Destiny Number. We will add the Name number and the Birth number, thus : 9 plus 9 equals 18. This is a double number, so we have to add 1 plus 8, which equals 9. Asha Singh's Destiny Number is also 9. Refer to 9 in the Destiny column on the following pages and read her indications.

Certain numbers have an affinity for each other, while other clash seriously. Even numbers harmonize with other even number and odd numbers harmonize with other odd numbers; but even numbers and odd numbers seldom harmonize except in the cases of 11 and 22. These two numbers are apt to be the exception and will harmonize with almost any other number. 11 is a higher octave of 2, because 1 and 1 equals 2; while 22 is a higher octave of 4, as 2 plus 2 equals 4. However, these two numbers are seldom reduced to 1 digit, because of their very strong individual power, therefore, when you have arrived at an 11 or a 22, you need not reduce it further but look in the indications that follow these pages for those two numbers.

We now propose to find out that whether Asha Singh with a Destiny number of 9 would be successful as a typist. Secure a number vibration of the word Typist. We find it gives us 2 plus 7, plus 7, plus 9, plus 1, plus 2, which equal 28. This is a double number, so must be added : 2 plus 8 equal 10. This likewise is a double number, therefore 1 plus 0, which equals 1. Since the word Typist responds to 1, which is an odd number the same as 9, Asha Singh would be a successful typist.

In the same way we can discover if she would be successful in Lucknow, Jodhpur, Trivendrum, or any other place, by working out the numerical values of such places. We can also find out if a certain street and number is favorable or not : if she should marry her lover or not; if travel by land, water, or air is best for her, etc., by securing the numbers of those things in the same manner we worked out her Name Number. Many other things will suggest themselves to you that you can work out for yourself or for your friends— such as the proper hotel to select, proper room number to engage, etc.

In figuring the numerical values of names, use the one by which the person is known. The name Ankur might have been given to a boy at birth but he always has been called Raj, which is a contraction of Ankur. In this case, use the name Raj. If you find the name Ankur produces better influences, he should immediately change his name to Ankur and sign it so at all times, insisting too that his friends call him Ankur instead of Raj. The name a person has been called all his life is the name vibration he responds to best, since its constant repetition has stamped upon his destiny the influence of that name, even though it be a nickname by which he has been called since childhood. Therefore, when numbering a name, the one by which the person is known is the one to be selected. By changing it, adding certain letters or spelling it differently, a new vibration is produced that will bring different results and a different personality if continued for a long enough time. Many famous people change the spelling of their name when they understand Numerology so as to create better number harmony.

It is sometimes best when a woman marries to retain her given name in addition to her surname. Sometimes it is best to drop the given name and use her husbands full name, placing Ms. before it. By working out the different combinations according to Numerology, the best combination may be found quickly and easily. Once a person decides to change his name, the old one must be forgotten entirely and never again used in any future dealings, introductions, or letters.

MISCELLANEOUS OPERATIONS WITH NUMEROLOGY

There are various ways in which Numerology may be employed to amuse or benefit the many who enjoy working out their numbers. The ideas presented here are just a few suggestions, others will come to mind as you work with the science of numbers.

SECURING FORTUNATE NUMBER WITH CARDS

Take a deck of ordinary playing cards and remove the 10 spots. Previous to this you will have worked out your Destiny Number of Asha Singh, which we found was 9. After removing the 10 spots and placing them aside, Asha Singh should shuffle the cards, give them one cut, then shuffle and cut them again. She should go through this operation of shuffling and cutting nine times. She should then deal off nine cards from the top of the pack and put them to one side. The very next cards should be turned up and placed face up on the table. If the card should be a 5, her Fortunate Number would be 5. If she is seeking a number with two figures, she should deal off nine more cards, place them aside and use the very next card, putting it face up alongside the first one. If she desires a number with three figures, she will deal off nine more cards and place the next one alongside the other two. Now suppose she had laid down the 5 of diamonds, the 2 of clubs, and the 8 of spades. Her Fortunate Number is 528. Face cards are to be considered as Zero or a Cipher. Therefore if the last card has been the King of Spades instead of the 8, the number would have been 520.

Remember always to shuffle and cut the cards as many times as your Destiny Number. If you have a Destiny Number of 4, you should shuffle and cut four times and deal off four cards from the top instead of nine. Your Destiny Number is the index to use. This process should not be repeated for the same person more than once in twenty-four hours because to repeat it destroys the vibration of the first fortunate Number and weakens the one found the second time.

Note : The reason the 10 spots were removed is a double number, and in Numerology you are concerned with digits or single numbers only.

TO FIND YOUR FORTUNATE YEARS

We wish to know if 1934 is a Fortunate Year for Asha Singh. Add 1934 thus : 1 plus 9 plus 3, plus 4, equals 17. Now add 1 and 7, which equals 8. This results in an even number, so it does not harmonize with Asha Singh's Destiny Number of 9; consequently, 1934 is not as fortunate for her as other years have been. The digit of the year must be the same or must be in harmony with your Destiny Number to be a Fortunate Year for you.

TO FIND YOUR FORTUNATE MONTHS

It is not necessary to work out the names of the months.

Merely consider the number of month : January, 1st month, therefore number 1; February, 2nd month, therefore number 2, etc. October is the 10th month, therefore 1 plus 0 equals 1. November is the 11th month and you always leave 11 as it is. December is the 12th month, therefore 1 plus 2 equals 3. Asha Singh's best month is the 9th month, which is September. If your Destiny Number is 3, you will have two good months—March and December, as both vibrate to 3.

FIND YOUR GOOD DAYS BY NUMEROLOGY

Any day which adds up to your Destiny Number is best for you. Asha Singh's lucky days in any month are the 9th, 18th and 27th. Her fairly good days are those which add to other odd numbers. The days that are neutral or slight adverse are those which add up to even numbers. Work this out with your own Destiny Number and check off your good and adverse days on your calendar to guide you.

TO FIND YOUR BEST HOURS OF THE DAY

Find the time of sunrise from your local daily paper or almanac. For example, suppose the sunrise at 6:15 A.M. The first hour after sunrise will be from 6:15 A.M. to 7:15 A.M. Marry Smith's best hours are the 9th hour after sunrise and any other hour which adds to 9, which would be the 18th hour after sunrise. These hours will vary a few minutes each day as the sun varies in rising time. Always use the hours after sunrise which equal your Destiny Number.

HOW TO CHOOSE PARTNERS OR FRIENDS

For best results in partnerships or friendships the Destiny Number should be the same as yours. Those who have Destiny Number not similar to, but harmonious, with yours will make fairly good friends, companions, and partners. Those who have Destiny Number which clash with yours will not make them good friends and the relationship will not be permanent nor very congenial.

HOW TO MAKE MONTHLY PREDICTIONS

Secure the Monthly Number of any month and year. (By Monthly Number is meant the numerical figure for any month reduced to a single digit.) Add it to your Destiny Number together, which is your Monthly Number for that month. Then refer to the Gallery of Numbers in the pages which follow for the general indications for that month. As an example, we will see what the indications for Asha Singh are for the month of June 1934 :

June	6
1934 add together	17
Destiny Number of Asha Singh	9
Total	32

3 plus 2 equals 5, which is her monthly Number for June 1934.

To find Asha Singh's indications for June 1934, refer to Gallery of Monthly Numbers.

Secure your own Monthly Number in the same way, using your Destiny Number instead of that of Asha Singh's. It will frequently happen that several months will respond to the same Monthly Number, but they will change from year to year.

The *Kitchen* should not be directly in front of the main door.

GALLERY OF NAME NUMBERS

1. The number of Creation, of Beginning, of First Impulses, or the Source of Energy. Persons whose name Vibrates to this number are trail blazers. Mostly all their lives they have been leaders and thinkers along pioneer lines, and they are usually popular in whatever sphere of society they choose to move. They are constructive in thought and like to be doing something new and out of the ordinary. They do not follow the path of others and generally have the courage to follow their convictions. There is a low level to this number also. Those who respond to this lower plane are eccentric, egotistical, haughty, dominating and self-conscious. If your name responds to this number, make every effort to overcome any weak tendencies that might show up in your character.
2. The number of Beauty, Culture, Truth, Perception and Consciousness. It is a decided feminine number and causes the person to respect and appreciate the refined and intellectual things in life. It is the number of cooperation, attraction, affection, emotion and enthusiasm. Those whose names respond to this number are warm friends, congenial companions, interesting entertainers and good judges of human nature. The lower plane of this number causes the person to be hasty, sensitive, and inclined to be too particular. If your name responds to this number strive to overcome any undignified tendencies that might show up in your character.
3. The number of Enlightenment, Thoroughness and Refinement.

This number causes a person to be tender, affectionate, sympathetic. Very cautious about details; prone to self-sacrifice and some idealistic principle and often willing to do assist friends. It is the number of the Holy Trinity and causes the person to be highly religious, impressionable, intuitive and magnetic.

4. The number of Realization, Security, Protection, Stability and Ambition. Those whose name responds to this vibration are true friends and good company. They possess brilliant and inventive minds and are inclined to reach a goal of their ambitions regardless of obstacles. They usually live a life of activity and variety and have many interesting experiences from which they learn much of the usefulness of life.

5. The number of Uncertainty, Hesitancy, Doubt, and Discouragement. Those whose name responds to this number will often become confused, restless, irritable, impatient and moody. They find it hard to form congenial companionships and frequently disagree with the opinions of others. They sometimes feel that life has been unkind to them—as though they were living an existence against which their nature rebels. If this is your name number and you feel that you do not want to fight against this influence any longer, it might be a good idea to change your number slightly so that it will respond to some other one. However, you can overcome it by exerting your will power if you keep on fighting.

6. The number of Dual Personality, Indecision, Temptation and Excess. Those whose names respond to this number have a peculiar nature. They are not always understood and very often are the cause of their own failures. If they will learn to gain from their experiences, they will make this a fortunate number ,but drifting through life will never get them anywhere. They like to follow the lines of least resistance and should overcome a tendency to indiscreet actions. Determination will help them conquer the uncertainties of this number.

7. The number of Spirituality, Mysticism, Wisdom and Success. Those whose names respond to this number are receptive, studious, creative and intellectual. They possess a deep understanding and desire the finer things of life. If there are no other conflicting influence in their numbers, they make warm friends, valuable employees and ideal companions or partners. They have a magnetic personality, are very unselfish and possess a rare outlook of life.

8. The number of Justice, Evaluation, Strength, Inspiration and Genius. Those whose names respond to this number have a strong personality. They are very magnetic, self-willed, independent, progressive, intuitive, and honest, candid and straightforward in dealings. The number 8 vibration is an extremely strong one, difficult to overcome. It causes a person to be very active, seldom contented for a great length of time, and eager for changes of events and scenery.

9. The number of Dominance, Efficiency, Psychic Consciousness, Humanitarianism and Renewed Energy. Those whose names respond to this number are clever, active, philosophical, and intuitive. They belong to the realm of prophets and possess an unusual telepathic mind. They have a fertile imagination, high ideals and are endowed with poetic or artistic abilities. They are usually very dignified and pleasant but odd and whimsical. They are refined, gentle, sympathetic and even tempered. They make friends easily and are quick to solve problems of others.

11. The Number of Power, Courage, Success, Adventure, Impulse and Energy. Those whose names respond to this number are merely an octave higher than those who respond to 2. They are deep thinkers and fond of exciting adventures. All times they are vague in their statements. Their minds grasp the general outcome or things but they usually skip details. The number has such a powerful influence that they often find themselves confused by many contradictions, likes and

dislikes. Clear thinking, determination, and concentration are qualities necessary to develop in order to control the restlessness this number creates.

12. The number of Rashness, Errors, Haste, Changeability. Those whose names respond to this number should overcome a tendency to be critical, restless and reckless. They often do not understand their own peculiarities. They say and do things on the spur of the moment and then wonder why they did it. They usually do not look before they leap. They are inclined to go to extremes, even against their own better judgment. They have a hard struggle with themselves, and it might be a good idea to change the name so as to respond to a better number vibration.

13. The number of Altruistic, selfless service, ministering, avatar, mystical, nurturing of the spirit, intuitive, emotional, protective, loving, teacher of teachers, crusader for justice.

This is the most influential of all numbers. It is the Master of Healing Love. When expressed to the fullest, the 13 lacks all personal ambition and instead focuses its considerable abilities toward the spiritual uplifting of mankind. What makes this number especially impressive, is the high level of sincere devotion. This is shown in its determination to seek understanding and wisdom before preaching to others. The 13 in full force is extremely rare. The 13 is on the journey of discovering its powerful healing energy through an open heart and unconditional love.

More open space in north or east gives name, fame and prosperity. Leaving more space on the south-west side in the house can affect the male member badly; whereas in industry it leads to financial loss and quarrel among partners.

GALLERY OF BIRTH PATH NUMBERS

(Secured from Year, Month & Date of Birth)

1. If this is your birth path, you will have many strange experiences. You will go through life making your own conditions and carrying out your own ideas. You will lead a constructive life.
2. If this is your birth path, you will seem to go around in circles and have repetitions of certain experiences at regular intervals. If you cultivate self-control, you will have an interesting, useful life.
3. If this is your birth path, you will enjoy many of the better things of life. You will travel much and gain from the experience of others. Yours will be a fortunate, contented life.
4. If this is your birth path, you will have many loyal friends. You will gain some prominence in the business or professional world. Yours will be a successful pleasant life.
5. If this is your birth path, you will have many strange experiences, at times difficult to overcome yet with your strong personality, you usually win out. Yours will be a long contented life.
6. If this is your birth path, you are apt to be too careless of your actions and general health and welfare. Success will be attained only through firmness of purpose and stability. Yours is a changeable but useful life.

7. If this is your birth path, you will undertake and usually accomplish big things. New and interesting experiences will present themselves. You will be the master of your own destiny. Yours will be an unusually successful life.
8. If this is your birth path, you will lead an active life but not necessarily a peaceful one. New ambitions will always spur you onward. Frequent outbursts of temper alter your course of life. Yours will be an adventurous career.
9. If this is your birth path, you will travel extensively, engage in unusually affairs and odd professions. Literature, art, music and the stage will attract you. Yours will be an interesting life.
11. If this is your birth bath, you will engage in many risky adventures. You will overcome obstacles by sheer force of will power. You are captain of your soul and master of your destiny. Yours will be a progressive life.
12. If this is your birth path, you will create many of your own difficulties. Losses may come through bad judgement or unreliable associates. Learn to think constructively and act with discretion. Cultivate self-control and you will succeed.
13. If this is your birth path, when expressed to the fullest this number lacks all personal ambition and instead focusses its considerable abilities towards the spiritual uplifting of mankind. What makes this number specially impressive, is the high level of sincere devotion. This is shown in its determination to seek understanding and wisdom before preaching to others.

Want to remain *healthy* ?

Remove medicine from kitchen & shift to living room.

GALLERY OF DESTINY NUMBERS

(Secured By Adding Name Number and Birth Path Number)

1. If this is your Destiny Number, you will achieve great success through your constructive efforts. Some help will be given to you, but you will be self-made.
2. If this is your Destiny Number, you will have many ups and downs in life, but through the aid of friends and relatives you eventually will be successful. You will have wealth if you utilize all your productive facilities.
3. If this is your Destiny Number, you will experience many successful ventures. The better things of life will assist you to the goal of your ambitions.
4. If this is your Destiny Number, you will have a life of usefulness, financial success and honor. Choose your profession carefully and forge ahead. Nothing can stop you if you persist. You will likely acquire much property.
5. If this is your Destiny Number, you will stand in your own way many times. Guard against accidents and do not trust stranger. Your life is one of varied experiences; some peasant, others discouraging.
6. If this is your Destiny Number, do not permit yourself to drift. Control your emotions and make the best of your opportunities; you are apt to overlook them. Success will come to you if you are alert and industrious.

7. If this is your Destiny Number, you may expect to attain prominence in life. Your light will shine far and you will travel extensively. Friends will be attracted to you.
8. If this is your Destiny Number, you will encounter financial difficulties often but usually will overcome them with experience and shrewdness. Your life will be very active.
9. If this is your Destiny Number, you will live a very useful, contented life. You possess many talents, are admired by friends, and enjoy an excellent reputation.
11. If this is your Destiny Number, you will lead a very active life, will succeed in big undertakings and be prominent in your sphere of life. You will be the master of your destiny and creater of your fortune.
22. If this is your Destiny Number, the lower qualities of your nature may control your life unless you strive to change them. Avoid schemes and questionable enterprises. Be deliberate in all projects. Overcome moods.
33. If this is your Destiny Number, you are on the journey of discovering its powerful healing energy through an open heart and unconditional love.Also, when expressed to the fullest, it lacks all personal ambition and instead focusses its considerable abilities towards the spiritual uplifting of mankind.

Do you want to retain the money in the house? Put a three leg frog facing his back to the main door for better saving.

NUMBERS AND COLOURS

Colours may be silent, but they are certainly not dumb at all. The language they speak is far more sweet, bright and eloquent. Like letter of the alphabet, they are also related with numbers. The numerical power of colour are quite a force to be reckoned with. Colour number shows the relationship of colours with their respective planets.

Colours are inseparable from life and existence. Life without colour is unthinkable. The vital role they play in our life, in the form of hues, tints and shades of our food, clothing, environment behaviors, feelings and attitudes, is an open secret. They are always with us. Wherever there is light and life, there are colours.

A colours is a sensation produced on our sense of sight, or eye by rays of light, when resolved by prism or by selective reflection. When there is no light, or a surface does not reflect any ray of light, black colour effect is the result. Similarly, white effect is produced by rays of unresolved light. Colours are in the form of intense vibrations causing colour sensation. Things appear to be coloured according to the colour of the rays they reflect.

A surface that appears orange, reflects red and yellow rays of light, which combine and give the colour sensation of orange. Similarly, when yellow and blue rays are reflected together, they produce green colour with their combination. Colour are warm and cool, exciting and sedative, soothing and stimulating, soft and coarse, deep and light, gaudy and simple. Colours influence our living in so many ways. They are closely connected with our behavior, temperament, mood and personalities. They cure, soothe, and satisfy us, when in harmony; irritate and cause gloom and nervousness when not in harmony. Our failure, success and colours are vitally interlinked. They are either in harmony or in conflict with our birth, name and other numerical vibration.

Colours have provided us with some finest expressions, and have thus enriched our language. Who does not wish to 'come off with flying colour?' He indeed deserves our praise, who could not 'change colour; in the face of a danger. An optimist is he who always 'paints things in bright colours'. 'Colour bar' is still there, a bane which spoils many a joy of humanity. Then, we have 'colour codes' and how important they are. Our regiments have their 'colour'. Colours stand for richness, variety, change, attraction and vitality of life and creation. We are all 'colourists' in one way or the other and show our true colour some time or the other.

Blue, red and yellow are called Primary colours, and orange, green and violet are secondary colours. All other colours can be obtained by the mixture and combination of these colours. For instance, red in combination with yellow gives scarlet, red with blue result in crimson, yellow and crimson orange, blue and yellow green, and so on.

The following chart of colours, show their effect and the things they symbolise :

	Symbol and Effect
Black	Melancholy, sorrow, death, gloom, evil, illness etc.
Blue	Peace, harmony, truth, serenity, thoughtfulness, hope etc.
Grey	Sobriety, Maturity, advancement of age and wisdom, resolution of conflict etc.
Brown	Gives a heavy feeling
Green Purple	Auspicious colour, inspires respect, growth, freshness, peace, nature, rest, etc.
Indigo	Balance, vitality, etc.
Orange	Warmth, cheerfulness, life, glow, plenty, glory, etc.

Red	Courage, excitability, anger, passion, war, strength, blood, love, creativity, happiness & force etc.
White	Truth, innocence, serenity, purity, joy, holiness, adds to peace, happiness and smooth environment etc.
Yellow	Stand for gaiety, joy and power.

Persons born on 1st, 10th, 19th or 28th of a month should wear and use brown, crimson, flame gold or yellow colours. Those born on 2nd, 11th, 20th, or 29th date should wear and use white, green or cream colours. Orchid, violet, pale, lilac and purple colours suit a number 3 person most. Indigo, blue grey and electric are the colours of number 4 persons. Number 5 persons should use only lemon, pink and all light shades especially grey and white as far as possible. Number 6 men and women are advised to make the maximum use of blue, rose, pink, scarlet (but not red) and henna colours. Brick red, lavender, violet, pale green, white, yellow and gold are useful for people born under the number 7. Number 8 people should use to the maximum such colours as dark grey, dark blue, black, purple, etc. Number 9 persons should make maximum use of rose, red, crimson, pink and purple colours.

The following chart shows the inter-relation between colours, planets and numbers :

Colours	Planets	Numbers
White	Sun	1
Cream or yellow	Moon	2
Violet	Jupiter	3
Orange or red gold	Uranus	4
Indigo	Mercury	5
Pale blue	Venus	6
Silver or opalescence	Neptune	7
Black	Saturn	8
Red or crimson	Mars	9

The signs of Zodiac are associated with the following colours:

	Signs	Ruling Planet	Colours
1.	Aries or Mesh	Mars	Red
2.	Taurus or Vrishabha	Venus	Pale blue
3.	Gemini or Mithuna	Mercury	Yellow
4.	Cancer of Karka	Moon	Green
5.	Leo or Singh	Sun	Orange
6.	Virgo or Kanya	Mercury	Dark green
7.	Libra or Tula	Venus	Pale yellow
8.	Scorpio or Vrashchika	Mars	Dark Red or Black
9.	Sagittarius or Dhanu	Jupiter	Purple
10.	Capricorn or Makar	Saturn	White
11.	Aquarius or Kumbh	Saturn	Blue
12.	Pisces or Meen	Jupiter	Grey

Colour therapy or cure through colours is now well recognized. To some colours the organs of our body react in a favourable way, while to others they show repulsion or disagreement. Colour vibrations effect the living organisms considerably in relation to their behaviour, emotions and defence mechanism. Sounds and colours are also associated and interlinked with each other. Certain sound vibrations respond well to certain planets and so also to certain colours.

'O' And The Compound Numbers

There are in all nine Planets in our Solar Systems, and, therefore, they are only Nine Primary or Basic Numbers on which all our calculation are based. All other numbers are just the repetitions of these numbers. A birth number is related to a planet having the same number, and it denotes the vibrations which operate throughout one's life. The birth number is always a single number. A Gross or Compound Number is obtained by the addition of birth date, month and the year. In the realm of occult interpretation and practice, Compound Number symbolize the potent or hidden powers of an individual, and often foreshadow his fortunes. Single or basic numbers are Personal Numbers and indicate what a person seems to be, his material sides, etc., but compound numbers show his spiritual aspects, his hidden powers. In association with basic number, the compound numbers can help you to draw a better ad fuller picture of your future life and events. Thus, you will have a brighter and fuller chart showing your general trend and current of life, your moral and spiritual strength, your latent powers along with your material and physical aspect. These numbers express the powers in your possession and your cosmic heritage, and how best and how often you can utilize them.

The Symbol 'O'

'O' symbolises infinity, the centre and a circumference, from which all things originate, and then finally merge back into it. It stands for Hiranyagarbha, the Golden Foetus, the self-existence or Infinite Boundless Being, the Universe in its entirety. It also stands for the Sun, the source of our life and existence. But our sun is only a representative of that Supreme, Eternal Sun which is the origin of love, peace, happiness, and all the other virtues we can think of. The Great Circle 'O' signifies nought, because he is nothing as well as everything and everything. He is in everything and everything is in Him. Thus, this paradox symbolises entirety, universality, happiness, health, power and at the same time emptiness, void, negation, loneliness, limitation, etc. But in numerological enumeration, nought is not counted, nor it is represented by any planet.

Rain water or drainage **should flow towards NE-East-North**

Compound Numbers

Number 10

This number symbolizes contentment, larger perspective, poise, tolerance, honour, self-reliance, confidence and success. The man under its influence realizes and utilizes his provided powers. The more efforts he adds the better and surer his achievements are. It is a lucky number in the sense that when desires and deeds are matched, there is no limit. On its negative side it would mean dependence, laziness and disrespect for others. He may be well known or notoriously known, the choice is his. It augurs well in every field i.e. in business, in love and romance as also in other walks of life; but one has to stand guard against its negative sides. As number 10 stands for a symbol of "Wheel of Fortune", one responding to its vibrations can do wonders if he realizes what he is.

Number 11

It denotes enthusiasm, intellect, inspiration, ideas and far better reach in the realms of Science, Arts and Spiritualism. On the negative side it symbolizes trials, tribulations, treachery from friends and lot of troubles for himself, parents and others. People responding to the vibrations of this number are generally misunderstood, and so become victims of other's misdeeds. If they get proper guidance, help and understanding, they can do remarkably well. Persons having this compound number should be vigilant and extra cautious about the hidden dangers and treachery of others.

Number 12

This number stands for ultimate success through struggle and strife. Once on the right track, the people with this number can achieve anything or any standard with perserverance and hard work.

Number 13

This number is supposed to be very unlucky, and so dreaded, but actually it is not so. It devotes Excessive Energy which is seldom channelised. It stands for change in profession, place and planning, it also symbolizes power, which if not used discreetly may result in destruction and ruin. Persons responding to this number can do well in business and industry, if they use their potentialities and power constructively in the desired direction.

Number 14

This number foreshadows dangers from forces of nature, movement, change, but is lucky in relation to money dealings, speculations and lotteries. Persons with this number can be quite successful as brokers, lottery agents and share agents. If this compound number is a result of computation in regard to future events and periodicity, one is advised to be cautious.

Number 15

It is a mysterious occult number but more associated with its baser sides than the higher aspects. Persons with this double number showing future events can stoop to any depth to serve their selfish ends. As a root or basic number reduced to 6, it is very lucky, powerful and auspicious, because then it is governed by Venus, the planet of love, beauty, perfection and passion. Persons with compound number 15 should have the business of luxury items, cosmetics, perfumes, decoration and furnishing, toys, presentation articles, etc. They should avoid by all means number 4 and 8 person and dates. Number 15 person make good and skilled artists, stage actors, singers and get ready cooperation from others on account of their personal charms and attractive manners. In this respect it is indeed a lucky number. In politics also such person have good chances of success, but they must be aware of sudden upheavals and turning of fortunes.

Number 16

It is a mysterious but at the same time a fatal number which foreshadows such calamities as accident, ruin, destruction and death. Thus, it is a very unfortunate number. It symbolises a tower struck with lighting from whioh a man is falling with a crowned head. As a compound number relating to future events, it forebodes ill, and proper precautions should be taken to avoid such grave consequences. Past the middle ages, people under the influence of this gross number are very likely to do remarkably well in the psychic field and may leave their names behind as thinkers, philosophers and numerologists.

Number 17

This number also shows fatalistic tendencies, and foreshadows personal and family troubles, strife and unhappiness. As regards material gains, it is certainly a lucky number. In business, especially dealing in machinery, metals and engineering goods, it leads one to success. Again it is fortunate compound number if it is not associated with such number as 4 and 8 and such dates. In the fields of occultism, spiritualism and thinking, person with this number can achieve greater heights.

Number 18

This number stands for conflict between the spiritual and material sides of a person, and ultimately the casualty on the former side. It foretells quarrels, strifes, unhappiness both in personal and family circles. It also foreshadows natural calamities and deception by others. As a compound number in relating to future events, it warns a person of dangers looming large and desires the need of greater precaution, care and proper planning to minimize the negativity.

Number 19

It is a fortunate and favourable compound number foretelling future events and life. A good deal of happiness, success, honour and bright career is associated with this number. Persons responding to the vibration of this number are sure to have much social esteem, personal gains, power and position. They come through with flying colours through times of crisis and test. In the field of love and romance also they can be sure of doing very well.

Number 20

This compound number in relation to future events, represents awakening, sound judgement and spiritualism. It is not a materialistic number at all; and awakening, realization, dynamism, etc., indicates in the field of religion and spirit. In the worldly sense, one can have success only after great patience and labour and it indicates delays, waiting and overcoming of difficulties by obtaining godly grace. A person with 20 as his compound number must seek strength from his spirit and its lord to have success in material world as well. Success is there but through struggle and strife in business and career.

Number 21

Compound number 21, is lucky and is associated with popularity, success, satisfaction, activity, honour and elevation. Whether in business or in service, such a person is likely to overcome difficulties easily. In the fields of love and marriage also, it betokens good fortune and success. It stands for sure victory, though sometimes through sustained efforts and labour.

Number 22

It denotes life of credulity, illusion and empty day-dreaming, resulting in disillusionment, repentance and much heart-burning. It symbolizes a good life gone to dogs because of malefic influence of others. Persons under this compound number in relation to future events should be extra cautious and should use their own wisdom and discretion. They should not be lead by their noses on any account. They should be more practical, rational and keep their feet firm on the ground. While taking decision proper deliberation, caution and consultation are most needed.

Number 23

It is one of the most favourable and auspicious compound number. It stands for success and fulfillment. Person responding to its vibration, are sure to get help, protection and guidance from their superiors and other persons in high positions. Persons and dates associated with numbers 1 and 3 are most favourable and promise best cooperation and help. They do remarkably well in the fields of education, research, science and technology. If this number occurs with root or single number 5 repeated twice or more, it ensures very smooth sailing and bright success in undertakings mentioned above.

Number 24

This compound number in relation to future events is also lucky, and foreshadows success, gains and possession of artistic tastes and likings. They obtain ready help from others in the hour of need, and in their turn help others sincerely. Fine arts, business in jewellery, fashion goods, furnishing and decorations, cosmetics, etc. are most suited to these people. It also indicates success and gains through love and cooperation of the opposite sex.

Number 25

It is a lucky number in the sense of future gains and successes. Under this compound number one gains through long and continuous experience, observation, efforts, and learning. Such persons are obviously self-made persons and their latter life, after middle aged. is far more happy, smooth and satisfying. They are more of an introvert and face uncertainties, strife, and struggle in the earlier part of their life. Patience, labour, courage and stamina are their obvious strength. These persons should take better care of their health, as it is likely to deteriorate because of continuous struggle in their lives.

Number 26

This compound number is relating to future life and events foreshadows ruin and disaster. The ill-thought of association with others is generally the basis of undoing in business and career. Such person should avoid contracts, partnerships and such dealing so as to involve other parties. If they undertake anything on personal judgement, good planning and work hard, success cannot elude them for long, but in family and personal life, privation, suffering and troubles are their lot. They are likely to be deceived in the matter of love and friendship as well.

Number 27

It is the fortunate number and denotes drive, initiative, power of command. As it symbolises the scepter it promises good results out of industry and investment. Persons in the shadow of this number are advised to try their own plans and ideas. 27 as a compound number in relation to future events is quite efficacious and ensures successful execution of plans and ideas of the native. Such persons should listen to others, seek their advice but ultimately they should stick to their own plans. In relation to marriage and family life, this number foreshadows a happy and prosperous life.

November 28

This gross number in relation to future events gives a mixed picture. It denotes a future full of promise but at the same time a future full of setbacks, instability and unfavourable change. If one takes extra precautions, one may succeed in guarding oneself against possible treachery, foul play and deceit. People responding to the vibrations of this number are certainly men of future promise, noble and industrious; yet they suffer loss and trouble because of their trust in others and always have a miserable beginning. Thus it may be termed as an unlucky number.

Number 29

Like the preceding, this one also denotes foul play, treachery, deception and breach of trust. It means unexpected troubles, privations and suffering at the hands of opposite sex. It foreshadows grief in relation to future events, and requires great caution and care on the part of the man. These persons have to be extra careful in choosing their partners both in life and business. If their other numbers are in harmony with this number, there is a fair chance of successful life.

Number 30

This double number in relation to future events denotes much of mental activity and less of achievements in terms of material success. The later half of their life is likely to be more smooth and happy. Persons born under the shadow of this double number are mentally superior, possess a charming personality and can make a mark even in early life, provided they are little more practical. It all depends on their mental outlook, and as such this number is neither lucky nor unlucky.

Number 31

This double number produces the similar results as that preceding one, but it is likely to heighten the loneliness, privation and melancholy of the native it represents. Thus, it is a quite unlucky number. Such person don't have even the touch of popular appeal and are financially very weak. Even for a modest amount of success they have to work very hard. Such people like change, travel and show themselves as superior to others in intellect and standard of living inspite of their comparatively poor financial position.

Number 32

This double number has the same influence and mysterious powers as the single number 5, or the reduced numbers 14 and 23. It is an auspicious number, provided the native it represents, hold to his own scheme, ideas, planning and judgement. People governed by this number can make very good leaders, diplomate, politicians and peace-maker. Their mass and popular appeal is never in doubt. They are warm-hearted, considerate and kind, but sometimes in the name of discipline or organisational success and unity they are likely to become hard and aggressive.

Number 33

This compound number is the most influential of all numbers. It is the master of healing love. This number combines the 11 and the 22 and brings their potential to another level. What makes the 33 specially impressive, is the high level of sincere devotion.

Number 34

The double number denotes the same significance as does the compound number 25.

Number 35

It has the same qualities as shown by number 26.

Number 36

It has the same qualities as the number 27 and foreshadows success and good fortune in relation to future events.

Number 37

This double number stands for fortune, friendship and love with the opposite sex. In relation with future events and life, it is indeed a lucky number. As far as business associations, partnership are concerned, it augurs smooth and happy sailing. In political field also a person under this number is bound to make his early and indelible mark.

Number 38

It has the same qualities as the number 29 and denotes general acceptance and successful life only with great care in choosing dealing with people.

Number 39

Has the same qualities as the number 30.

Number 40

It has the same qualities as the number 31, which is one of its own series of compound numbers.

Number 41

It is a lucky number and possesses all the qualities as does the number 32.

Number 42

Has the same meaning as does the number 24.

Number 43

It is obviously unfortunate double number and foreshadows upsets, upheavals, strife, ruin and failure.

Number 44

It reveals the same meaning as do the number 26.

Number 45

Exhibits the same tendencies as the number 27. It is undoubtedly a fortunate number and symbolises energy, drive, initiative and fruitful activity.

Number 46

It is a lucky number and denotes the same meaning as 37.

Number 47

It has the same meaning as 29.

Number 48

Has the same meaning as 30

Number 49

It has the same occult meaning as number 31.

Number 50

It symbolises the same thing as does the number 32.

Number 51

It is a very powerful number symbolising good luck, love, success and rapid advancement in military, political and business fields. In relation to future events it is a lucky number, but a person possessed of the number should guard himself against accident, treachery and attempt on his life, etc. In the affairs of love and matrimony also it indicates a satisfying relationship.

Number 52

Reveals similar qualities as number 43.

These 52 double numbers represent the 52 weeks of the year, and there is no need to go beyond this point.

HORARY

Hours and approximate time		Sunday	Monday	Tuesday
DAY	6am 1	Sun	Moon	Mars
	7am 2	Venus	Saturn	Sun
	8am 3	Mercury	Jupiter	Venus
	9am 4	Moon	Mars	Mercury
	10am 5	Saturn	Sun	Moon
	11am 6	Jupiter	Venus	Saturn
NOON	12am 7	Mars	Mercury	Jupiter
	1pm 8	Sun	Moon	Mars
	2pm 9	Venus	Saturn	Sun
	3pm 10	Mercury	Jupiter	Venus
	4pm 11	Moon	Mars	Mercury
	5pm 12	Saturn	Sun	Moon
NIGHT	6pm 13	Jupiter	Venus	Saturn
	7pm 14	Mars	Mercury	Jupiter
	8pm 15	Sun	Moon	Mars
	9pm 16	Venus	Saturn	Sun
	10pm 17	Mercury	Jupiter	Venus
	11pm 18	Moon	Mars	Mercury
MID-	12pm 19	Saturn	Sun	Moon
NIGHT	1am 20	Jupiter	Venus	Saturn
	2am 21	Mars	Mercury	Jupiter
	3am 22	Sun	Moon	Mars
	4am 23	Venus	Saturn	Sun
	5am 24	Mercury	Jupiter	Venus

GRAPH

DAYS

Wednesday	Thursday	Friday	Saturday
Mercury	Jupiter	Venus	Saturn
Moon	Mars	Mercury	Jupiter
Saturn	Sun	Moon	Mars
Jupiter	Venus	Saturn	Sun
Mars	Mercury	Jupiter	Venus
Sun	Moon	Mars	Mercury
Venus	Saturn	Sun	Moon
Mercury	Jupiter	Venus	Saturn
Moon	Mars	Mercury	Jupiter
Saturn	Sun	Moon	Mars
Jupiter	Venus	Saturn	Sun
Mars	Mercury	Jupiter	Venus
Sun	Moon	Mars	Mercury
Venus	Saturn	Sun	Moon
Mercury	Jupiter	Venus	Saturn
Moon	Mars	Mercury	Jupiter
Saturn	Sun	Moon	Mars
Jupiter	Venus	Saturn	Sun
Mars	Mercury	Jupiter	Venus
Sun	Moon	Mars	Mercury
Venus	Saturn	Sun	Moon
Mercury	Jupiter	Venus	Saturn
Moon	Mars	Mercury	Jupiter
Saturn	Sun	Moon	Mars

After determining the length of the day, divide it by 12 to obtain the duration of each planetary hour of the day. Say on a particular day the sun rises at 6.45 A.M. and sets at 6.22 P.M. It makes the duration of the days to 11 hours and 37 minutes, which when divided by 12, gives the duration of 58 minutes and 5 seconds of each planetary hour. On this particular date, suppose a person is born at 9.30 A.M., and suppose that day is Monday. It means that person's planetary day is Monday and planetary hour Jupiter.

The Zodiac, a belt of heavens limited by 8° from the ecliptic on each side, is divided into 12 equal parts called Signs of Zodiac. These signs in numerological order are—

1. Aries or Mesh
2. Taurus or Vrishabha
3. Gemini or Mithuna
4. Cancer or Karka
5. Leo or Singh
6. Virgo or Kanya
7. Libra or Tula
8. Scorpio or Vraschika
9. Sagittarius or Dhanu
10. Capricorn or Maker
11. Aquarius or Kumbha
12. Pisces of Meen

The Sun makes an orbit of the Zodiac in 365 days, 5 hours, 48 minutes and 45 seconds. So, there are three years in succession of 365 day each, and the fourth of 366 days, known as the leap year. This leap year, every fourth is thereto make for the difference of 5 hours and about 49 minutes each year, making about 23 hours in every four years.

The actual and exact time of the sun's entry and exit from a particular sign of the Zodiac may be ascertained from astronomical almenc or ephimeris. The approximate date of the Sun's entry into these 12 signs of the Zodiac are as under

Signs	Date of Entry
1. Aries	21st March
2. Taurus	21st April
3. Gemini	21st May
4. Cancer	21st June
5. Leo	23rd July
6. Virgo	23rd July
7. Libra	23rd August
8. Scorpio	24th October
9. Sagittarius	23rd November
10. Capricorn	21st December
11. Aquarius	20th January
12. Pisces	19th February

These above dates showing the Sun's entry into the sign are approximate, and if your birth date happens to be on 21st March, or 21st April, or 23rd August, or 19th February, and so on, the best course would be to consult the ephimeris of the year to find out the exact hour and date of the sun's entry into a particular sign at the time of your birth.

The Seven Planet rules over the 12 signs of the Zodiac as under :

Sign	Planet	Sign	Planet
1. Aries	Mars	7. Libra	Venus
2. Taurus	Venus	8. Scorpio	Mars
3. Gemini	Mercury	9. Sagittarius	Jupiter
4. Cancer	Moon	10. Capricorn	Saturn
5. Leo	Sun	11. Aquarius	Saturn
6. Virgo	Mercury	12. Pisces	Jupiter

Thus, the Sun rules over Leo the 5th sign of the Zodiac, the moon over cancer the 4th sign, Mars over Aries and Scorpio the 1st and 8th signs, Venus over Taurus and Libra the 2nd and 7th signs, Mercury over Gemini and Virgo the 3rd and 6th signs, Jupiter over Sagittarius and Pisces the 9th and 12th signs, and Saturn over Capricorn and Aquarius the 10th and 11th signs. Some modern astrologers like to assign the rule of Aquarius to Uranus (4) and that of Pisces to Neptune (7). These two planets Uranus and Neptune have their own significance, but relatively they are still less known, and so their study and inclusion in numerology do not form a part of the basic knowledge.

The Sun, the central planet of our solar system, while in different signs bestows different characteristics on the natives born in various signs. His own sign is Leo, the fifth sign of the Zodiac.

As the different position of the sun bestows different characteristics on different persons born in different signs, similarly the different locations of the rest of the planets like Mars. Moons, Saturn, Jupiter, Venus and Mercury also causes the changes in temperament, nature, fortunes, health, mental make-up, economic and other achievements, etc. of the natives.

We have already seen that the day at the first hour begin from the local time of the sunrise, and the first hour is ruled by the planet giving its name to the day. If the sun rises at 6 A.M. the first hour upto 2 P.M., and so on. Therefore, it follows that a person though born on Monday may have the prominent characteristics that of Venus, because this planet was in ascendancy at the time of his birth. So, a native may show the marked characteristic of a different planet because of his different planetary hour, in which that particular planet happened to be strong.

Inter-relationship of different planet at the time of a native's birth indicates the relative strength and weakness of each planet and that marks the individual's fortunes. Each native has his or her Destiny Number corresponding to the Ruling Planet. As we have already seen a previous chapter, this is arrived at by adding the date, month and the year together. This figure based on complete and full birth date is likely to give us a more comprehensive picture of the native fortunes. The association and combined effect of the various planets in a birth date reveal the total and comprehensive chart of a man's future events. Let us take a man, born on 18.10.1921. We add up the date, month and the year to determine his Destiny Number and the presiding Planet.

Date 18 = 1 + 8 = 9

Month 10 = 1 + 0 = 1

Year 1921 = 1 + 9 + 2 + 1 = 13

This gives 5, as Destiny Number, and Mercury as the Presiding Planet. With the help of further enumeration, analyse the following table, showing the association of various planets can be drawn :

Date of Birth 18-10-1921

Destiny Number—5 (Mercury)

1 'Sun	8 Saturn
9 Mars	2 Moon

Here the Destiny No. 5, and Presiding Planet Mercury have been shown at the top of the table. The first planet Sun (1) is placed in column one and the next Saturn (8) in the second column. The third planet is again Sun, and it is marked with a stroke ('). The fourth planet is again Sun and it is marked with a second stroke. Then there is Mars (9) with the Moon (2), placed in the next line and in their respective columns, and again in the end there recurs the Sun (1), and so we mark it with a third stroke. It marks the completion of our Horary-table.

We see that the sun (1) recurs 3 times, and in all there are four Planets—Sun (1), Saturn (8), Mars (9) and Moon (2), Mercury the Presiding Planet, bestows upon the native an attractive personality, good intelligence and artistic taste. He may achieve remarkable success as a writer, teacher, journalist, scientist or as a businessman. The well marked recurring influence of the Sun, is an additional advantage, but then the combination of the planets are very unfortunate. There are as many as four Suns, but they are adversely affected by the powerful and malefic Saturn. This is certainly an unfortunate association. Again the Mars-Moon combination is also a bad one. The conjunction of Mars and Moon foreshadows family unhappiness and financial troubles. Therefore, in spite of Presiding Planet Mercury (5) we cannot foresee a happy and fortunate life for the native.

Let us take another person, for instance born on 3.9.1921, and draw his Horary table :

Date 3 = 3

Month 9 = 9

Year 1921 = 1 + 9 + 2 + 1 = 13

Compound Number 25 = 2 + 5 + 7

Date of Birth 3-9-1921

Destiny Number 7 (Moon)

3 Jupiter	9' Mars
1' Sun	2 Moon

The Destiny Number 7 (Moon) clearly indicates all round progress, popularity, adaptability and success of the native.

The dominant double Mars (9) in conjunction with Jupiter (3) foreshadows a remarkable career either in military or politics. If he enters business, he is likely to head a big commercial organisation. This happy combination foretells of a double or recurring Sun over others. The next combination of the double or recurring Sun (1) and the Moon (2) indicates that the man must shine and come to possess a very good reputation. He should rise to a very high position in life and acquire large gains. The unreduced or Compound Number 25, in relation to future events foreshadows strength, favour and good luck.

Now, it is obvious that the character and fortune of a given person can be very well deciphered with the help of the Horary-table prepared on the basis of his complete birth date. Thus, in relation to both character to luck revelation, the importance of the Horary-table can hardly be over-emphasized.

The following chart can be of great help in determining the happy or unfortunate effects of various planet combination :

Planet	Combinations	Result
Sun (1)	Moon, Mars, Mercury Jupiter, Venus and Vice Versa	Fortunate
Moon (2)	Jupiter, Sun, Mars, Mercury Venus and Vice Versa	Fortunate
Mars (9)	Jupiter, Sun, Moon, Mercury, Venus and Vice Versa	Fortunate
Mercury(5)	Jupiter, Sun, Moon, Mars, Venus and Vice Versa	Fortunate
Venus(6)	Jupiter, Sun, Saturn, Moon, Mars, Mercury and Vice Versa	Fortunate
Saturn(8)	Venus and Vice Versa	
Saturn(8)	Moon, Mercury, Jupiter, Sun, Mars and Vice Versa	

Let us take one more example of some person known to history, say Shakespeare born on 3.5.1564

Date 3	= 3
Month 5	= 5
Year 1564 = 1 + 5 + 6 + 4	= 16
Compound Number	= 24= 2+4 =6

Date of Birth 3-5-1564

Destiny Number 6 (Venus)

3 Jupiter	5 Mercury
1 Sun	6 Venus

4 Sun

The Presiding Planet Venus and the Destiny Number 6 symbolise a great magnetic personality, determination, high aesthetic sensibility, great artistic ability and popularity. This number is in complete harmony with his birth number (3).

Jupiter (3), the planet of ambition, top position, discipline, conscientiousness, self respect, in combination, with double Mercury foreshadows creative writing of high degree, good fortune and authorship. And then conjunction of sun and Venus is again a very happy association, and denotes combination of various artistic talents and accomplishments.

DEFINITIONS

Name Number—The number secured by transferring the letter in a person's name to numbers from the Table on Page 72. This shows the general characteristics the person has developed from the use of the name through life.

Birth Path Number—The number secured by transforming the Month, Date and Year of the person's life and the outstanding events to be experienced.

Destiny Number—The Number secured by adding the Name Number and Birth Path Number together. This shows whether your name adds or subtracts to your Birth path indications. If it hinders you, the name should be changed for the future.

Name Numbers remain the same always, unless you change the spelling of your name. Birth Path Number never change; they always remain the same. Destiny Number remain the same unless you change the spelling of your name.

CONCLUSION

In this book the author has attempted to give you the simplest method of Numerology known. After fifteen year's of practice with the science of name and numbers, he had found this system to be reasonably accurate for the amateur, whether he studies Numerology as a hobby and pastime or for personal gain.

The indication given in the Gallery of Numbers are flexible and can be slightly altered or shaded to suit different individuals. The exact words may not be used, but the important part is that you retain the substance of the good or bad indications in interpreting your numbers or those of your friends.

We present this work for what it may be worth to the layman for amusement or practical use. Many people find this an interesting party game. As such we offer it to the public, waiving any claims as to its infallibility.

LOSHU - GRID

(Laxmi - Yantra)

We should now learn something about LOSHU square. Chinese gives equal importance to Loshu square as they do for the pa-kua. It is derived from Laxmi Yantra, similar to the one on the back of a tortoise considered to be the 2nd incarnation of lord Vishnu. The square consists of numbers one to nine set in a square.

As you can see from the square whether you add the numbers vertically, or horizontally or diagonally the sum of the numbers of 15.

The square is also called magic square and is believed to give important information while analysing the building/ destiny of the person.

Let us have a closer look at the square and try to see its significance.

	15		15		
	SE	SOUTH	SW		
	4	9	2		
EAST	3	5	7		WEST
	8	1	6		
	NE	NORTH	NW		
	15	15		15	

Number1	Represents	Water element
Number 2, 5, 8	Represents	Earth element
Number 3, 4	Represents	Wood element
Number 6, 7	Represents	Metal element
Number 9	Represents	Fire element

How to apply the loshu grid.

Lets take an example of Birth date of 12th July, 1977 :-

Place the number of Date of Birth in the loshu square as shown :-

	SE	SOUTH	SW	
		9	2	
EAST			777	WEST
		11		
	NE	NORTH	NW	

Now we can observe that

(A) In the chart 3 & 4 (Represents wood element) is missing thereby growth is missing in his life.

How to get Cure : Green light in the east and southeast sectors to fill up 3 & 4 (Wood element) in his office, pre-energised green pyramid in East & South East in bed room for enhancing growth.

(B) Number 5 & 8 (Represent Earth element) is missing thereby whatever he speaks or acts will not be forceful, thereby he is not properly rewarded in the life.

Cure : Yellow bulb in the centre of the room and he has to wear crystal neclace and a peak himalayan mountain wall poster painting to be decorated or fixed on the South Side Corner 2' wall and West Side Corner 2' wall thereby creating South-West Corner with 2 mountains in his bed room and office. Keep green stone pyramid in South West for strength & stability.

(C) Number 6 (Represents Metal) is missing in the chart which means he is missing friends or helpful people. He has to struggle independently for his development in life or corner.

Cure : To wear a yellow metal bracelet on the hand or any yellow colour metal watch strap on the body to get helpful friends-perhaps ladies will not have this problem, as they wear golden Bangles. Hang a 5 rod yellow/golden wind chime in N/W sector & place a pre-energised yellow pyramid in NW.

Note : In the present chart No. 3, 4 & 8 in one line are missing by which this person will always be feeling shy to demand any thing in his life.

The table on the next page shows how we can find which element is missing in one's date of birth and how to cure it.

No.	Direction	Element	Solution
1.	North	Water	Keep ornamental water fountain/ fish aquarium.
2.	South-West	Big Earth	Hang high peak mountain poster without water/wear Crystal Neclace/ Pendant, wear pearl ring. Keep green stone pyramid.
5.	Centre	Earth	Hang high peak mountain poster without water/ wear Crystal Neclace/Pendant, wear pearl ring, Keep green stone pyramid, Hang a yellow bulb in centre of the room.
8.	North-East	Small Earth	Keep ganga kalash filled with Holy ganga water, wear crystal neclace /pendant.
3.	East	Wood	Light green bulb, keep picture of greenry/energized green pyramid

No.	Direction	Element	Solution
4.	South-East	Wood	Light green bulb, keep picture of greenry, energized green pyramid.
6.	North-West	Metal	Wear watch with golden metalic chain, hang 5 rod metalic 11" golden/yellow wind chime, install energized yellow pyramid
7.	West	Metal	Wear watch with silver metalic chain, hang 5 rod metalic 11" silver/white wind chime, install energized white pyramid.
9.	South	Fire	Light red bulb, install energized red pyramid.

•••

DIAMOND BOOKS
NEW PUBLICATIONS
CURE IN 72 HRS DIABETES Type I & II
YOGA For Mind, Body & Soul
51 SHAKTIPITHAS
Suresh Kumar Singh
Autobiography of a Yogi
Paramahansa Yoganand
INTERNATIONAL BESTSELLER SELF HELP GUIDE
THE POWER OF YOUR SUBCONSCIOUS MIND
DR. JOSEPH MURPHY
PERFECT SUCCESS Mantras
Dr. Ramesh Pokhriyal 'Nishank'
TRUST HARD WORK NOT DESTINY
Dr. Ramesh Pokhriyal 'Nishank'
Dreams that don't let you Sleep
Dr. Ramesh Pokhriyal 'Nishank'
Workplace romance? Try it and get...
Screwed
Varun Singh
The Time Machine
Homo Sapiens Version
Monarch Srivastava
Love after break up is it possible?
Prakash Goenka
Wealthy Inside Wealthy Outside
An holistic approach to become Real Rich
Harsha Garg
The Power of Good Manners!
Pankaj K. Singh
Are We Ready for Change
Pankaj K. Singh
DREAM BRIDGES SUCCESS
Tishya Shree
Dr. Ramesh Pokhriyal 'Nishank'
Inspiration for the World
Indian Culture, Civilization & Traditions
DIAMOND BOOKS
X-30, Okhla Industrial Area, Phase-II New Delhi-110020
Tel : 91+11-40712200 email : sales@dpb.in www.diamondbook.in

SELF HELP

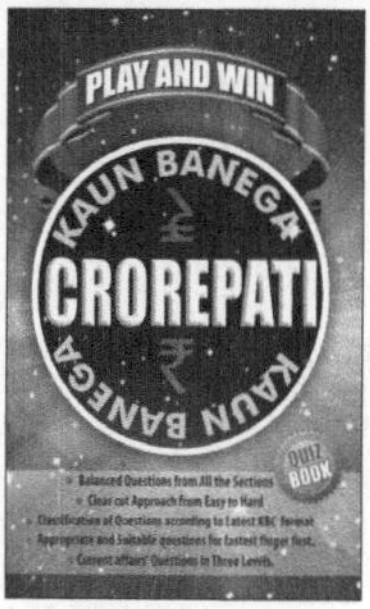

DIAMOND BOOKS X-30, Okhla Industrial Area, Phase-II New Delhi-110020
Tel : 011-40712200 email : sales@dpb.in

Shop online at www.diamondbook.in